Belonging

A resource for the Christian family

Published by
The Baptist Union of Great Britain

A Resource for the UN
International Year of the Family

GW01417725

© Baptist Union of Great Britain, April 1994
ISBN 1 898077 36 3

Layout: John Parnaby
Cartoons: Linda Francis
All statistics are taken from *Social Trends 24* (1994) unless otherwise stated.
Photographs have been acknowledged wherever possible.
Back cover photograph © John Twinning.

Printed by Stanley Hunt Printers Ltd, Rushden, Northants.

Contents

Foreword

When you are rich, when you have a name, when you have friends, or when you are a member of a respected group, you are never really oppressed. When in difficulty, only a telephone call and everything is fixed. I know this myself; I've never been poor in this way as I have enough friends and contacts. When you have no friends, when you are an immigrant and speak the language badly, you are quickly oppressed, for you cannot defend yourself. This is true of people who have a mental handicap, the sick, the disabled, the prisoners and all those who have no voice. They are the oppressed ones and they are numerous in our society. There are many without work, with no security, living off meagre wages, living day by day in unbearable situations of fear and anxiety, with children sick or other dependents. We all know these situations. Each of us has met them; they are in the cities, they are all around us. But what is frightening is that the disciples of Jesus are so frequently in comfort. On which side of the road is Jesus? On which side of the road are his disciples?

Jean Vanier

This study guide on the theme of Belonging takes seriously Jean Vanier's challenge and calls Christians to enlarge their understanding and vision of God's purpose for human community and 'family'.

But it is more than a study guide; it is a resource pack which enables that enlarged understanding to find expression in practical action, both individual and collective.
Following five chapters dealing with general principles, the book examines the theme in relation to ten specific issues, including marriage, parenting, multi-cultural living, disability and unemployment.

Many people have contributed to this book and we are particularly grateful to the following:
(in alphabetical order)

Ron Ayres	Joan King
Faith Bowers	Colin Marchant
Danny Brierly	Nick Mercer
Jill Davies	Jack Ramsbottom
Stephen Finamore	Philip Robinson
Bryan Gilbert	Roy Searle
Jane Grinnoneau	Derek Tidball
Linda Hopper	John Weaver
Iain Hoskins	Haddon Willmer

Edited by: Anne Wilkinson-Hayes & Paul Mortimore

Notes on using Belonging

Belonging can be used by an individual, much in the way Christian Training Programme (CTP) manuals have been used in the past. However, its main strength lies in its use with small groups.

The leader needs a full manual, but group members need only have photocopies of the worksheet at the end of each chapter. These can be copied free of charge for use in churches.

The leader of the group needs to select a number of chapter headings which are of particular relevance to the group. It is suggested that a couple of the general overview chapters (1-5) are used before dealing with some of the specific issues.

Leaders should then thoroughly familiarise themselves with both the text – which includes many supplementary questions, as well as important facts and figures – and the worksheet.

It is very important to note that the worksheets contain more material than it is possible to get through in an average evening meeting. The leader must therefore be selective prior to the event and choose questions that will be appropriate for the specific group ensuring a balance of affirmation, challenge and practical steps forward. Group members should be encouraged to pursue the remaining questions in their own time, or the group could decide to take an extra week.

Each worksheet begins with lists of materials and any preparation needed by the leader. In some sections, eg, Young People, preparation some weeks ahead is necessary to ensure the best activities for the group. Each worksheet also ends with an individual practical commitment space. Adequate time should be allowed for this to be filled in by group members, and for prayer.

The material can also be used as the basis for a church conference or weekend away, where different groups can study different sections. The ideas for worship can be used in small groups or in services when the theme of Belonging or family church is being explored.

We very much hope you will enjoy using this material and that it will benefit our life and witness as churches.

Belonging &

SOCIETY

Starting with an overview of changes in current British society, this chapter explores ways in which Christians may both understand and confront the growing sense of alienation in our neighbourhood and nation.

THE SITUATION

'FAMILY AND FRIENDS TOP OF THE LEAGUE – THE REST NOWHERE' ran a headline comment on a UK survey on relationships at the end of 1993.

In varied spheres such as work, politics, neighbourhood, leisure activities, nationalism and religion many people are dramatically losing their sense of identity. If people feel they belong anywhere it is now almost entirely in the privatised, personal worlds of family and friendships. Even in these areas traditional patterns are disintegrating and loyalties are weakening. What is happening in our society? What factors are changing our attitudes? Can we see the consequences? How do Christians, so often talking about belonging, respond to these current trends?

▶ Do you agree or disagree with this analysis? Think of examples/stories which support your response.

FACTORS

The factors contributing to the changes are both external and internal. External forces, movements and processes link up with inner shifts in values, convictions and commitments.

These factors include:

Population Mobility. Many of us move away from places and people. Neighbours alter, areas change. New people(s) arrive. Each shift cuts roots and removes ties but also gives new opportunities.

Life Expectancy. This means that either relationships have to survive longer or when one partner dies there can be a very long period of loneliness for the surviving partner. It is unlikely that families will remain in the same neighbourhood throughout a person's lifetime, so pensioners can become geographically separated.

Youth Culture. This has become more sophisticated and complex, and so increases the sense of alienation – 'another generation', 'not of my time'.

Economic Turmoil. Long before the recession raised unemployment (leaving workers bereft and cut off) and intensified poverty (cutting out hospitality and limiting the visit to the pub), industrialisation had moved families on from their

John Twinning

homeland and split the home from production. Few now spend a lifetime with one employer. Most will change jobs and even transfer to other skills or professions.

Pluralism. Areas like East London are now multi-everything: race, faith, colour, language. There are new faces and new ways. "Everything has changed around here. I don't belong any more." Culture clash and diversity of lifestyle are now features of the UK urban landscape.

Structural Change. Those institutions that gave shape and stability to social life appear to be under question. The NHS, trade unions and local councils shake under reorganisation, recession or political policy. Even time-honoured national institutions like the monarchy and the established church are in transition.

▶ *How do you respond to this sense of massive upheaval?*

How do you personally cope with all the social changes around you?

How do you think the church copes?

Question of Identity. It is not only Baptists who have questions about identity! Who are we? Anglo-Saxon or European, Christian or secular, black or white, male or female? We are not sure where we belong – or who really belongs to us.

Acceleration. The pace of change is hotting up. We find it hard to accept or absorb. Waves come at us more frequently, they are higher and are from many different directions. Alvin Toffler's prophetic book, *Future Shock*, has come true. We feel out of joint, out of touch and out of control. So we want to either 'return to basics', that is be seduced by nostalgia, or 'pull up the drawbridge' and opt out.

THE CONSEQUENCES

The consequences of these social changes are all around us and often etched deep within us. On one side, we have 'commitment-phobia' and diminishing relationships. On the other hand, we have a 'choice-culture' and a massive variety of options.

Commitment-phobia. Politicians use this phrase in the face of falling party membership and shrinking contributions. Religious leaders see it as an explanation for falling membership and poorly attended meetings. Experts point to the reluctance to marry (or to get engaged!) and the divorce figures as evidence of a fear of commitment to the deepest of all relationships.

Behind it lies disillusion and a cynicism springing from a sense of impotence and a rejection of long-held standards.

▶ *Where do you see 'commitment phobia' and where do you identify it in your life?*

Fewer Relationships is the reality for many.

A local community unit carrying out a survey of relationships within an Anglican parish uncovered three clear trends:

- people did not know their neighbours – even by name!

- few had links with community groupings – whether that be church, pub, club or agency.

- most had little sense of belonging to the locality – having moved in or planning to move out.

And this in an area that once prided itself on neighbourliness and belonging.

The Choice-culture. A massive range of choices face us in our supermarket culture and our consumer-oriented way of life. The vast array that competes for our attention leaves us, as consumers, confused and uncertain. One example of this is in the area of relationships. 'Arranged marriages' may be the accepted way in the Indian sub-continent, but teenage girls in the UK struggle for personal choice. Parents may be uneasy or disapprove of sexual relationships outside of marriage, or of homosexual relationships, but more and more young people 'belong' through cohabiting, or 'come out' as gay or lesbian and belong to a subculture. We pick and choose according to our likes and dislikes. Words like duty, responsibility and tradition sit uncomfortably with current social values.

The Opportunist Society. The slogan *We've never had it so good* has, for many of us, become *We've never had it so varied.* Instead of belonging to a football club or a cricket team we can take part in a range of thirty sports. The fish and chip shop has become one of a cascade of fast food, national cuisine take-aways (sixteen in our local main road!). Mainline political parties compete with fringe and pressure groups, action cells and global movements. Belonging to Friends of the Earth or Greenpeace, for example, is seen as more interesting than attending the local Labour Ward meeting. And we all know about the variety of churches – charismatic or reformed; new or traditional; elder-led or ministerial.

How would you rate the sense of belonging in your local area on a scale of 1-10?

How would you go about more accurately confirming this hunch?

THE CHALLENGE

In the middle of all this stand the Christian churches. Are we aware? Are we afraid? Or are we responding?

We have to acknowledge that denominational allegiances are weakening, membership standards are often dropping and churches are in danger of becoming one subculture among many. The challenges may be immense but the opportunities are similarly great.

The Bible has contemporary relevance. We are called to:

Understand afresh the Incarnation. God with us. 'The word became flesh' is the foundation stone of the gospel. 'Belonging to…' means becoming one with the people of today, whoever they are, wherever they may be, and however they may live.

Be the Body. 1 Corinthians 12 sets it out. We are to be one body, sharing as members, contributing our gifts, growing as we relate together. 'All of you are Christ's body, and each one is a part of it.' This is the model of human life under God. Where that happens individuals will be drawn and bonded together.

Demonstrate the Kingdom in worship, witness and word. The church and its members are the visual aids that show in action and attitude that believing, being and belonging are for real.

Hold the Vision that 'every knee shall bow' (Phil 2:10) and 'all will be one in Christ' (Gal 3:28). All other belongings are interim or incomplete.

Pray the prayers of belonging, whether that be the Family Prayer – 'Our Father' (Lk 11), the High Priestly Prayer of Jesus – 'I pray that they may be one' (Jn 17) – or the Pastoral Prayer of Paul to 'the Father, from whom every family in heaven

What, ideally, does the church have to offer to a disintegrating society?

Does your church feel that a significant part of its mission is to build Kingdom values into the society around it, and enable people to have a greater sense of belonging and wholeness?

and on earth is named' (Eph 3:14ff).

Whether you are thinking about the nature of the church, wrestling with the shape of a human family, working with the disadvantaged or lonely, or concerned about what is happening in our society, you need understanding. Look hard at the factors that are bringing about change and add to the list. Face the consequences – negative or positive. Work together with other Christians to respond in the way that Jesus did to the world of his day – and now to our own.

PRACTICAL IDEAS

COMMUNITY SURVEYS

Many churches think that they know their area, but in fact when a detailed survey is conducted they are often amazed by the findings. A church in Exeter thought it knew that what was needed in its locality was a youth centre. But a door-to-door survey revealed that there were nearly 200 families living in vastly overcrowded conditions, often in just one room, and that what was really needed was a family centre with space for children to play, a room where parents could have a little quiet away from their children, and some good laundry and drying facilities.

A community survey is an excellent way of determining both the changes that are taking place in the neighbourhood and how people are responding to them. It may be that whilst the social profile of the area has changed markedly, these changes have not been reflected in the church. It may be that people are struggling with specific issues that the church is unaware of because the membership is drawn from a catchment area other than that around the church.

It is important to be clear about what you want to know, so that you can ask the right questions. Often surveys that purport to be finding out about the local community are really excuses to ask people about their religious views, and these do not necessarily reveal an accurate or useful picture of the neighbourhood. Are you interested in how people feel about the area, or discovering gaps in what the neighbourhood provides?

The BU Social Action Office can supply a list of surveys currently available, and can send some samples for review. Greg Smith (at the Community Involvement Unit, Durning Hall, Earlham Grove, London E7 9AB) has done a great deal of work in this area and can supply much information. It is also available in electronic format as text files for customising, if churches send him blank disks.

Notes to leaders
You will need some large sheets of paper and felt pens. It may also be useful to have some examples of community surveys for people to look at. Contact Greg Smith at the address in the text or the BU Social Action Office.

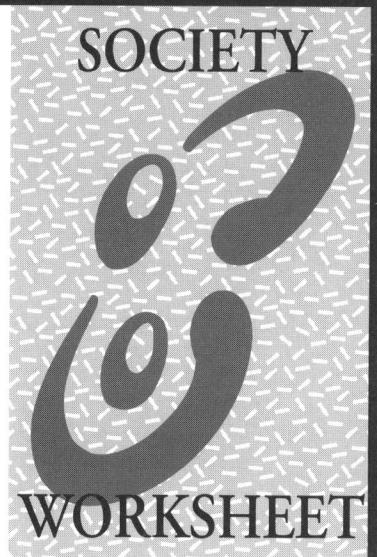

1 *'The sense of belonging in society at large is crumbling.'*

☐ I agree with this statement   ☐ I disagree

Think of some examples or stories to illustrate your response and share these with the group.

2 List as a group, on a central piece of paper, factors that might contribute to a sense of disintegration within society.

3 When you look at this list what do you feel?

☐ Fed up   ☐ Angry

☐ Scared   ☐ Powerless

☐ Excited by new possibilities   ☐ Amazed

☐ Nothing very much   ☐ Other ....

● Why?

4 Share examples of how the church responds to changes in society. What changes have you noticed affecting your church in the last ten years?

5 Social changes have many consequences. 'Commitment-phobia' has been identified as one way we respond to this upheaval.

List groups/organisations/classes/relationships in which you are involved. Now score your level of commitment to them on a scale of 1-5. Try to identify some reasons for the score.

List	Score	Why

Belonging

5 cont
- Why do you find commitment difficult in the areas you score low? Share, if you are able to, your answers with the group.

- Do you think 'commitment-phobia' is a reality in society today? What effects does it have?

6 Most of us would say that choice and opportunity are important aspects to life. But is there a negative side, when these choices and opportunities multiply so rapidly? What is it?

7 How would you rate the sense of belonging in your local area? Mark a position on the line below.

Strong Sense ●————————————————————————————● *No Sense of*
of Belonging   *Belonging*

- How would you go about more accurately confirming this rating?

- What role do you think your church plays in strengthening this sense of belonging, or otherwise? Should the church make a difference to a local community, and if so, how?

8 Discuss the steps towards your church doing a community survey of your area through which you could accurately understand the changes that have happened and how people feel about your locality?

> **One practical thing I resolve to do as a result of this study is .....**

9 What other information would you like to have about your area that could help the mission of your church?

Belonging

Unlike other sections, the material here is presented entirely as a worksheet – intended for use in small groups. It can form a useful general introduction to the more specific issues and ideas explored later in the book.

I Read the following quotes about church life. In the empty boxes, jot down some evidence of your own that shows Christians are less than perfect in creating a sense of belonging. Share your examples with the group.

In my first church I remember being told the reason the gallery was not carpeted was because that was where the workers worshipped. The carpeted area down below was strictly for those in a higher station in life (James 2:1-4).

A minister a year out of college and in his first church meets a colleague at the college reunion and bemoans his lot: "I know where I'm going. If some members are not happy they can leave and go somewhere else."

A young girl who makes a commitment to Christ is baptised and comes into membership. A couple of years later she no longer attends. On being asked why, she says that Sunday mornings are spent helping a handicapped cousin: "I feel closer to God doing that than when I worship in church."

On Mothering Sunday they handed out daffodils in the church – one was proferred to me and then whipped away – "you haven't got children have you?" they smiled. It felt like adding insult to injury.

Mrs Jones has worshipped at her local church for many years but now feels increasingly isolated. Her sight isn't as good as it was and her favourite hymns, the ones she knows by heart, are never sung; the Lord's Prayer is never said and the outside world is never considered.

Since her divorce Mary has noticed a cooling of the atmosphere towards her in the church. Some members have made it quite plain that divorce is wrong for Christians and there is talk of taking her out of the Sunday School because she would have a bad influence on the children.

2 Read the following passages. On a central piece of paper, list the marks of the early church.

eg: *Acts 2:38 Belonging was expressed in a personal relationship with Christ. Only by belonging to Jesus can we belong to others.*

(NB There may be several features within each passage)

Acts 2:38-47	Acts 4:23-24	1Cor 10:16-17	2 Cor 8:1-4
Acts 13:1	1 Peter 2:9	1 Tim 5:3,16	

● Now add another piece of paper and, against your list above, identify how **your** church expresses these marks of the early church. Note any aspects that are missing or are weak. Discuss possible reasons for this.

You should end up with something like this:

3 Write down all the different groupings in your church eg, young/disabled/older/married/single/male/female/black. Beside your list indicate whether or not they feel they belong, and whether the church actively affirms them.

● Think of features in the church's life which you think either affirms and supports them, or marginalises and discourages them.

Groups	Belong (Y/N)	Features of Church Life that:	
		Affirm	Marginalise

4 Many people, both within and beyond the church, are confused, broken and hurting. Do you think that the church can really be a community that both reveals an alternative way of living and transforms the society around it?

● Where do you see this happening in the ministry of your church?

● What has to change in your church in order to see this happen more effectively?

Belonging

5 List the activities of your church: worship, prayer meetings, youth group, etc.

• Look at each activity. How inclusive is it?

• Do any people feel alienated by it and why?

• Go back to the list you made in question 3 – is every group catered for?

• What else would be worth exploring?

• Represent these activities as named circles on a large sheet of paper or use the page overleaf.

Your leader will now provide you with 50 x 2p pieces. Allocate them to the activities proportional to the time the church, as a whole, gives to them (roughly): eg, if the bulk of church life centres around planning and participating in the worship, then this gets, say, 20 coins; if hardly anyone ever goes to the prayer meeting, that gets just one!

• Mark those that are oriented towards the wider community. What proportion of the church life is given to these? Are there many coins here?

• What does this tell you about how your church is creating a sense of belonging?

One practical thing I resolve to do as a result of this study is .....

Belonging

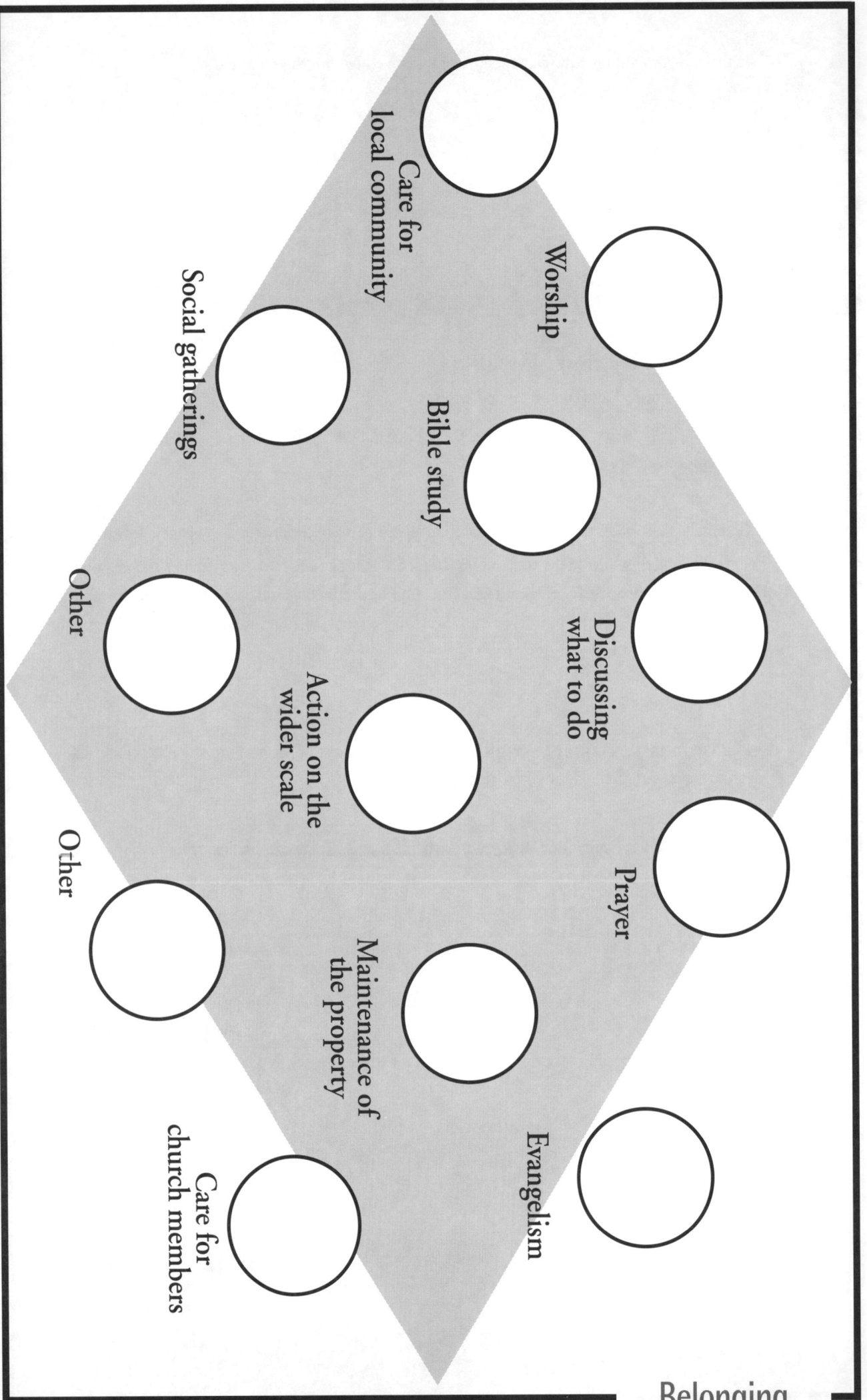

Care for
local community

Worship

Social gatherings

Bible study

Discussing
what to do

Other

Action on the
wider scale

Prayer

Other

Maintenance of
the property

Evangelism

Care for
church members

Belonging

THE BIBLE

Given our present unease with the family as it is, perhaps it is opportune to take a fresh look at what the Bible teaches about belonging. To do so will call into question whether the call for the reinstatement of the traditional family is all that the Bible advocates. The following gives an overview of all the main material. Specific issues will be looked at under other chapter headings.

God's seven-fold verdict on the world he had created was that 'it was good' (Gen 1:4, 10, 12, 18, 21, 25, 31). The first thing he ever declared to be 'not good' was the man's solitariness (Gen 2:18). To overcome the loneliness Adam felt God created a companion for him (Gen 2:20-25). Human beings were made for relationship.

God's concern to provide satisfactory relationships for people is affirmed throughout the Old Testament. 'A father to the fatherless, a defender of widows is God in his holy dwelling. God sets the lonely in families ...' (Psa 68:5-6, see also Psa 146:9). To be surrounded by company and to enjoy the blessing of laughter, play, marriage, children and commerce with others is seen as a sign of God's blessing (Psa 127:3-5; Isa 54:1-3; 62:4-5; Jer 33:10-13). Conversely, for a person to be deserted and a place to be left desolate was a sign of God's displeasure (Psa 69:25; Jer 6:8; 7:34; 10:22; 25:11-12; 44:22).

We are made to be in community – in 'family', although the Bible means something different by that word than we do. The family is not simply a biological or social structure but has theological significance. It is the place of God's covenant activity, and the means through which God chooses to bring blessing to the world (Gen 12:3 RSV). It is the place where teaching about God is to be given and the experience of God is to be nurtured. (Deut 6: 4-9; 11: 8-21; see also 1 Cor 7:14.)

We will look systematically at what the Bible has to say under the headings of Old Testament, Gospels and Letters.

OLD TESTAMENT

The Old Testament has no word which corresponds to our word 'family'. By 'family' we usually mean a two-generational unit composed of mum, dad and the children, which is relatively isolated either from other generations, ie, the grandparents or great grandparents, or from other relatives, neighbours, colleagues and friends. The closest the Old Testament gets to 'family' is a word which means 'house' and this usually refers to something much bigger than our 'isolated nuclear family'. The groups to which 'house' refers were people bound

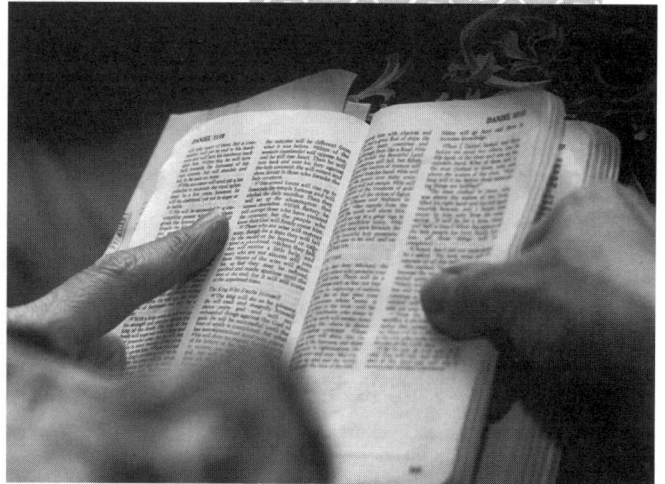

together by ties of blood and who shared a common dwelling. The word was fluid and could refer to the whole 'house of Israel' or to a tribe, clan or household.

People did not define themselves as individuals, nor as nuclear families, but perceived themselves as part of a much larger extended family. The story of Achan illustrates this. Joshua 7:16-18 shows that although Achan was married with his own children (v24), he was seen primarily to be a member of the tribe of Judah, of the clan of Zerah and the household of Zimri, his grandfather. A similar picture is given of Saul in 1 Samuel 9:1-2.

We've come about the job

Advantages of the Old Testament Model of Family

This large inclusive unit could easily incorporate 'aliens or strangers' who did not belong by blood ties. It was also much better adapted than the isolated nuclear family to bearing the burdens of children and their upbringing, of the sick, mentally ill, or otherwise needy. Family obligations were strong. Not only was it their duty to defend the honour of the family but to provide support when needed. Out of this concept of solidarity grew the practice of the 'kinsman-redeemer.' If a family member fell into trouble and had to sell himself into slavery, other members of his family were expected to come to his rescue (Lev 25:25, 47-53). In the event of a husband dying, his brother was encouraged to marry the widow in order to provide for his name to continue (Deut 25:5-10). The most beautiful outworking of that principle is found in the story of Ruth (3 & 4). A less happy example is found in the story of Tamar in Genesis 38.

Aliens and Strangers

Special stress was laid on the duty to incorporate immigrants into the community through embracing them in the extended family. They were to be treated with respect and dignity and not to suffer any discrimination. (Lev 19:33-34.) Whatever their racial background or social circumstances they were to be treated as one would treat one's neighbour (Lev19:18), always remembering that the Jews themselves had once been displaced persons until, by God's grace, they had been set free (Deut 10:17-19). Their children were to be given the same advantages as the native born (Deut 31:12-13), especially in regard to their knowledge of God. Love and respect was not to be a mere facade but to arise from the heart (Lev 19:17-18).

Other disadvantaged groups such as the economically poor, the disabled, the blind and the elderly were also to be shown respect, provided for and in no way marginalized by the fit and well-to-do in society (Lev 19:9-10; 14, 32).

How does the way we organise family life today in Britain enable us to absorb others, or respond to others when they are experiencing stress?

Within the New Testament the 'family' is only mentioned on a few occasions. The lack of more frequent references is a reminder not to transfer unthinkingly the teaching of the Bible regarding families to our own day. We need to enter fully into the culture of the Bible's times before making application to today.

The more usual word relates to house or household and refers to an extended family rather than our isolated nuclear families.

Having said that, family situations and household affairs often form the background for the parables of Jesus (eg, Matt 7:9-11; 18:23-25; 21:28-32; 22:1-4 and Lk 15:11-32).

An Ambivalence about Family

We also get a glimpse of Jesus' own family – the fullest glimpse we get of any family in the New Testament. Mark's Gospel does not present them in a very positive light and Jesus seems to live and act independently of them (Mk 2:1; 3:31-34; 6:4). Families are a likely source of opposition for the disciples (Mk 10:29-30; 13:12-13). This leads to Mark stressing the need for disciples to leave their families and to find among those who do the will of God their true family (Mk 3:35; 10:29-31). The church, then, was to become an alternative family.

Luke presents Jesus' family in a much kinder light from the beginning of his Gospel, where Mary is portrayed as 'highly favoured' (1:28), to the end, where Jesus' brothers are in the upper room (Acts 1:14). But the same themes are evident in Luke as in Mark. Families can be a hindrance to disciples, even hostile to them (Lk 9:57-62; 12:52-53; 15:25-27; 18:29-30). The true family of God are all those, no matter what their natural family situation might be, who do the will of God (Lk 8:19-21). Such teaching reminds us not to exalt the family beyond its due. Some Christian talk about the family gets close to idolatrous. (See further, J A Walter, *A Long Way from Home: A Sociological Exploration of Contemporary Idolatry*, Paternoster Press, 1979, ch.3.)

Some Christian talk about the family gets close to idolatrous.

A Special Place for the Marginalised

Throughout his ministry Jesus has a special place for the marginalised, be they lepers (Lk 17:11-19); a demon-possessed man condemned to live among the tombs (Mk 5:1-20); an unclean woman who was not fit to be in a crowd, let alone touch a man (Mk 5:25-34); a grieving widow who had lost her son, and so her means of livelihood (Lk 7:11-17); an out-and-out tax collector called Zaccheus (Lk 19:1-10) or a number of women who though probably of independent means needed healing (Lk 8:1-3). All these he healed or in other ways provided them with shalom and enabled them no longer to be outcasts but integrated into their families, their communities or the band of disciples.

Among the marginalised particular note should be taken of the single. In the Old Testament singleness was virtually unknown (Jeremiah is an exception, Jer 16:2). The Jews considered it a duty to marry and there was something distinctly suspect about a man if he did not do so. But Jesus completely re-evaluates the status of the single, both by remaining single himself, although being the most complete and fulfilled human being that has ever lived, and by teaching the value of singleness for the work of the kingdom (Matt 19:10-11). No longer was singleness imposed by others, by birth or by circumstances. Now it could be seen as a positive choice before God for which he would give his grace. So, single people could take their place alongside others in the new family of God.

THE LETTERS

The chief social unit mentioned in the rest of the New Testament was the household. These were composed of parents, children, servants and other dependants such as employees, freedmen or friends. The authority in the household would reside with the lord, master or father. Major decisions, such as which God to worship, would be taken by him and its members would follow in his footsteps. Once more we must remember that people in New Testament days did not view themselves as isolated individuals in the way we do today, but defined themselves in relationship terms. So a choice might be made by someone else but still be authentic.

Households became the major building block of the early church

They were the platform for mission (eg, Acts 16:14-15; 18:1-4, 7-8); the unit of conversion (Acts 10:23-48; 16:31-34; 18:8; 1 Cor 16:15); the locus of worship and teaching (Acts 2:46-47; 20:20; Rom 16:5; 1 Cor 16:19; Col 4:15); the arena of fellowship and the means of collective stability and personal growth. The frequent references in the letters to 'one another' make most sense when set in the context of household life and worship. The church saw itself as the household of God (Eph 2:19; Gal 6:10; Heb 3:1-6).

Christians are referred to as the Children of God, that is, the grown-up and fully participating children of a heavenly father (Gal 3:26-4:7), who are born or adopted into God's family (Rom 8:16-21; 9:8; Phil 2:15; 1 Pet 1:14; 1 Jn 3:1-2). It is from this imagery that the church has fallen into the way of speaking about itself as a 'family' – but the word needs to be used with care since to speak of believers as all children of God is not quite the same as to say that we are the family (in the contemporary sense) of God. The former is an inclusive description, embracing all people whatever their natural family situations, the latter is exclusive and sometimes hurtful to those who are not members of a present day nuclear family.

The Church: A Home for Misfits

The early church embraced within it those who often did not fit or carry any weight in normal society (1 Cor 1:26). It provided a home for misfits (1 Cor 6:9-11), having cleansed and transformed them in the power of the gospel. It provided new significance for the single (1Cor 7:8-9, 25-35). It provided a new status for slaves (1 Cor 7:22-23), women (Gal 3:28) and those from pagan and unsophisticated cultures (Col 3:11). All of these found that they could take their place on a level with and alongside the most orthodox, and respectable, Jewish male who had been converted to Christ. They all belonged to God and had a place in his household of faith.

THE BIBLE: A CHALLENGE FOR TODAY

Contemporary society often has tunnel vision. Belonging means to be a member of an isolated nuclear family. If people do not belong there they often do not fit. But the isolated nuclear family is a fairly recent historical invention. The Bible has a rather wider view of family and usually uses the word house or household to describe it. Within the wider structures the once married, the not yet married and the never to be married have their place and play their part as valued members of the community. It presents to us a great vision of shalom where all are integrated within the community and with their God and all find delight, work and fulfilment in satisfying relationships.

Notes to leaders
You will need Bibles, large sheets of paper and pens.

1 Read Gen 2:18-25. What do we learn here about basic human needs?

Individuals in the group should look up one or more of the verses listed below.

Psa 68:5-6   Psa 127:3-5   Psa 146:9   Isa 54:1-3

Jer 6:8   Jer 7:34   Jer 10:22   Jer 25:11-12

Jer 33:1-13

● What do they tell us about our humanity?

Combine your findings on a central piece of paper.

2 In the Old Testament 'family' is never used. People saw themselves belonging to much bigger units – tribes or clans (cf: Jos 7:16-18; 1Sam 9:1-2).

Can you think of the advantages of an extended family network?

Look up Lev 19:33-34; Lev 25:25, 47-53; Deut 25:5-10; Ruth 3-4.

3 How does the way we organise family life today in Britain either hinder or help us in absorbing others, or responding when others are experiencing stress?

4 Read Mk 10:29-31 and 13:12-13.

What do these verses tell us about the tension between loyalty to our natural family and loyalty to the fellowship of God's people?

Carol, at church, says to you that she cannot do any pastoral visiting – "I must put my family first".

● How legitimate is this in the light of the passages from Mark?

● How would you reply?

Belonging

5 Fill in the following tables in pairs and discuss your answers with the rest of the group.

Read the following texts	In what ways were the people mentioned marginalised in their society?	How did Jesus respond and help them to 'belong'?
Mark 5:1-20		
Mark 10:13-16		
Luke 7:11-17		
Luke 8:1-3		
Luke 17:11-19		
Luke 19:1-10		

● Why has the church largely shyed away from following Jesus' ministry to the outcasts and most needy?

Who are the marginalised today? (list)	How might Christians respond to their needs?

6 In the New Testament, decisions were often made by one member but were accepted by the entire household. There was a strong sense of mutuality and corporate responsibility for a network which went beyond the nuclear family. Where do you see this happening today?

● To what extent do we think about the impact our 'private' or family decisions might have on the wider community?

● Where do we draw the lines?

One practical thing I resolve to do as a result of this study is .....

7 *The early church embraced within it those who often did not fit or carry any weight in society (1 Cor 1:26).*

What evidence is there in your church that it is a genuine and inclusive house of faith, where all can belong on equal terms, whatever their occupation, skin colour, gender or financial status etc?

● What other evidence would you like to see?

Belonging

23

Belonging &

FAMILY VALUES

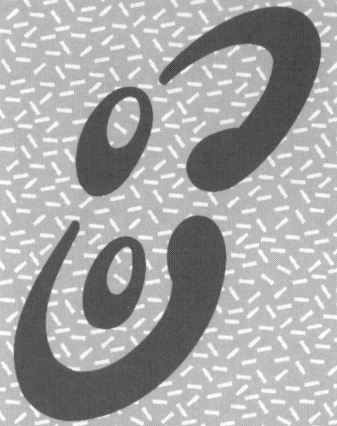

The current call from the government to return to basics, especially in relation to personal and family values, sounds high-minded and sensible. But what should Christians make of this summons?

This chapter asks some fundamental questions about 'family values' and explores a challenging theology of belonging. Paradoxically, we discover that our primary belonging to God involves some inevitable separations.

We have deliberately chosen the title 'Belonging' rather than 'Family' for this book. Even when they are not in family human beings want to find strength and joy in belonging to someone or something. Family is one common social form of belonging, but it has no monopoly. Can anyone be found who is so absorbed by family that they belong to nothing and no one else? Such people are rare and not likely to be happy.

Why 'Belonging'?

Talking about belonging touches more than family. It helps us to deal with what concerns people when they speak of traditional family 'values'. Talk of values may indicate that our thinking is not tied to one form of family, like the nuclear family. Rather, speaking of values enables us to identify and point to the good things that people often seek, work at and sometimes realise and enjoy in and through their families. Caring for people in daily practice, really loving one another, for instance, may be a basic *general value* people want to achieve. Whether it is institutionalised in one way or another does not matter, so long as the essential value is being realised in interpersonal relationships. 'Belonging' is a word which may sum up all sorts of *positive values*: loving, respecting, being reliable, supporting through thick and thin, learning from and working with one another, rejoicing with those who rejoice, weeping with those who weep.

Belonging is Natural and Problematic

Belonging is what human beings seem to desire and to need, at least for survival. Belonging is natural, universal and necessary. That much seems clear from ordinary observation and experience. It fits with what is commonly believed by Christians about God. Our desire to belong is said to be innate because God created us with it. Our primary belonging is to God the creator, but it is then to be expressed and explored in our solidarity with the rest of humanity and with all creation. As God the Trinity – three belonging to one another in perfect love – is social, so we, created in the image of God, develop institutions and ways of life that involve people in belonging. Our human forms of belonging, like family, church and even, maybe, nation, workplace and club may

What institutions do you 'belong' to ?
Do they help or hinder your belonging to God?

enable us to experience 'godlike belonging', or these belongings may obscure the primary call to belong to God. In human communities people can experience God's grace, be nurtured and grow to wholeness in loving relationships. Too often, however, these communities and their institutions become substitutes for belonging to God and too much is expected of them. The more mere human community is affirmed and emphasised, the more we overload it. Because belonging is natural and universal, we cannot avoid searching questions about whether our ways of belonging are true to God and practicable for human beings.

BACK TO TRADITIONAL FAMILY VALUES ?

Some people believe that family structures and relationships are in deep trouble, even terminal disintegration. Many people are hurt, their lives derailed, their spirits distorted in these crises. Pain and worry tempt us to shout loudly for simple and urgent solutions: so the people clamour to government, government lectures the people and sets up the Child Support Agency, and the media hammer away on all sides.

The churches are often under pressure from government and media to call people 'back to traditional family values'. Some churches are happy to oblige. They believe God is the solution for social problems, and they are eager to show that the faith of the church is relevant to felt human needs. So they are glad when politicians want churches to reassert tradition and family in a straightforward and uncompromising way. But if the church were wise in faith rather than anxious to prove itself it would investigate the invitation before it responded to it. It would try to avoid acting on theologically simplistic diagnoses. There are questions to be asked.

▶ What do you understand are 'traditional family values'? What family values have most helpfully shaped your life?

Why the Concentration on Family?

What can families achieve when society as a whole is disordered? Why is it assumed that churches have a special responsibility for family order and well-being when so few families go to church?

Is the family a solid institution in our society in which everybody is – or could be – integrated? Is the family available as an effective and universal form of social discipline and organisation? In some societies, central government and local administration are parts of a hierarchy that runs down to village elders or the wardens of apartment blocks, who maintain order at a local level. Is family, for us, the most local and basic unit in this hierarchy of social order?

Can we work realistically with such a vision of an ordered society? Can enough people be expected to submit to the necessary disciplines to make it workable? Could a government legislate consistently to uphold the family as the practicable basic unit of society?

▶ Is it possible for governments or any institution to legislate for family values? Why?

Given that we are swimming, possibly drowning, in a society disordered from above as well as from below, by respectable power as well as by criminal deviance, by intellectual confusion as well as by malevolence, it is foolish to expect that the family can rescue us.

The family is, and will continue to be, more a barometer of our troubles than an escape from them.

At best, the family is one fragile and only occasionally successful form in which people hold on to and help each other through this troubled life. The Christian affirmation of family must therefore be quite different from the anxious demand for social order: it is a mixture of order and disorder, in which people live this present life, colliding and co-operating with each other, struggling to love and be loved while living through all the failures and frustrations of love. The sensible Christian does not look to the family for solutions to the problems of life.

'Back to ...'

What golden age do we have in mind? Can even the oldest members of our churches remember a time when families were problem free? If there was ever adequate order and uniformity in family structure, how much did that depend on coercion, ignorance and fear? Few families in Victorian times were divided by divorce, but many were devastated by early deaths, especially of mothers, by internal conflicts covered by respectability and don't leave aside the exploitation, the child labour, the hunger and bad housing.
O where is my wandering boy? was a singable hymn in Victorian times.

That past experiences of family were often bad does not allow us to claim to have made progress; it merely shows that we are still facing the same issues and there is no good past to go back to.

Which Family?

When we talk of 'traditional family values' which family do we have in view? Is it the extended family, where several generations, many aunts, uncles and cousins live together? Or is it the nuclear family of parents and children, in a house or flat with no room for anyone else and far from grandparents and other relatives? It is fashionable in our culture to want to get away from the nuclear family which lacks the wide variety and manifold interactions possible in the extended family. For some, belonging to church expands the nuclear family into an enlivening network, an extended family resting on baptism not on blood relationship. Is such a church a universal model? Some, however, who live in extended families are critical of them: they foster hierarchy and conflict. There is no perfect family form any more than there is perfect church order.

In Britain now, more than ever, it is misleading to talk of the traditional family. There are many traditions. There are European and Caribbean and Asian patterns of family. Households made up of a married couple with dependent children are much more common among those from the Indian, Bangladeshi and Pakistani communities. In 1992, over a half of all Indian, and nearly two thirds of all Bangladeshi and Pakistani households, were a married couple with dependent children, compared with only a quarter of households from the white, West Indian and Guyanese communities.

Families differ because of class and gross variations in wealth: families are affected by economics. Since churches have little economic power, they should

The family is, and will continue to be, more a barometer of our troubles than an escape from them.

Right! You're staying in until you've cleared that mess off the walls

not allow themselves to be drafted as decisive custodians of family life and structure. Or, to put the same truth positively, churches that care about families should attend to the economics of family forms and address their challenge to the powers which determine the economic conditions within which families are formed and broken. Churches should not accept that there is an immediate direct connection between faith and family in our society. To link one with the other adequately, churches must work in concrete detail with the economic, cultural and political realities of our society which influence what families can become. It is a dangerous delusion for churches to think that, by championing the family, they can be socially useful and yet escape the pains of politics.

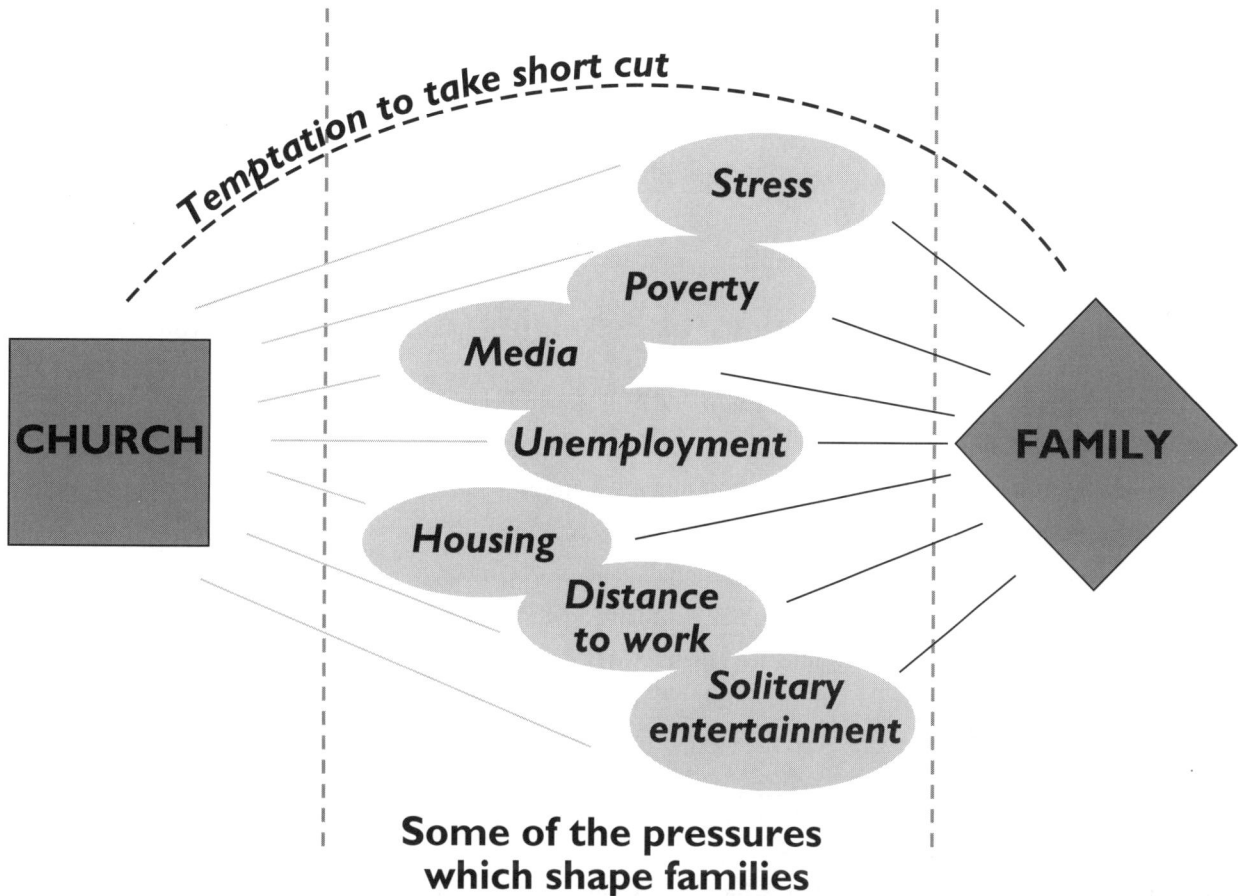

Temptation to take short cut

CHURCH

Stress

Poverty

Media

Unemployment

Housing

Distance to work

Solitary entertainment

FAMILY

Some of the pressures which shape families

A THEOLOGY OF BELONGING ?

Belonging and Family Values

From whatever angle family is probed we gain the same set of insights: family is an important focus of human living together. It is what many people invest their lives in and often get pain and problems and disappointment as the major return.

It is the disillusion with family life at present that has precipitated the current focus in media attention. What are the roots of this dissatisfaction?

Being Antisocial

Dissatisfaction with family and society may express our unsociableness, our refusal to belong and to pay the price of love and justice and order. We want to get away from the commitments that hem us in. We do not like living in families

27

or other circles where someone else has got us sewn up. Wanting to have a chance to be ourselves, we find that others have decided who we are before we knew what was happening (we are named beings). Fed up with belonging, we become militant individualists: we will use others when convenient but we will not belong to them. There is always a justified and necessary resistance to slavery, but it can be a cloak for sinfully refusing to belong.

Looking to the Future

Alternatively, this dissatisfaction with present forms of social involvement may be a sign that we are seeking a 'city which has foundations' (Heb 11:10) where at last – but only at last – we can belong and really be at home, where positive values are no longer mocking, teasing ideals but are lived and unbroken reality.

Any genuine Christian view of belonging starts with this dissatisfaction.

The Central Christian Theology of Belonging

Christian faith thinks in terms of God the Creator and so looks for belonging as God's gift in creation. But Christian faith does not think of human belonging as an unbroken, undistorted reality, coming directly from the hand of God to us. What we receive is indeed the good creation of God, but in receiving it, it is distorted, so that it does not automatically serve human good or display the unobscured glory of God. Families and all human belonging, even the best examples, share in what is sometimes called the fallenness of creation. That does not mean there is nothing of value and nothing to hope for, but that nothing is perfect or perfectly secure; even the best will show in some way that it shares in the 'falling short' (Rom 3:23) of our present humanity. Even the strongest is vulnerable to being overwhelmed by evil.

Any serious Christian approach to belonging starts at the Cross. On the Cross, God reaches out across the gulf of sin and alienation and chooses to belong to his human creatures at great cost (Rom 5:8,10).

Belonging in the Christian view is not primarily the natural connectedness given us by our first createdness; it is the commitment to being reconciled with enemies, to making new connections across divides, which we are called to in the new creation in Christ.

Loneliness

The crucified Christ to whom Christians say they belong was and remains a very lonely figure. In faith, he endured (with some protest but not excessive surprise) desertion by his friends, only to come then to the devastating loss of fundamental belonging: 'My God, My God, why hast Thou forsaken me?' (Mark 15:34).

► Are you disillusioned with family life?

Why? Is it to do with personal issues or wider issues or temperament?

► Read John 1:11 & Rom 5:8-10. What are the implications for those of us who follow Christ in creating belonging for others?

Let him who cannot be alone beware of community. Let him who cannot be in community beware of being alone.

Dietrich Bonhoeffer in Life Together

Christian faith tackles the problems of belonging within the light shed by this darkness of God. Belonging is not found without wrestling with loneliness. The Bible is as much about separations and hostilities as simple belongings.

Forsaking all other

The lonely Jesus can be seen as a passive victim of human wickedness which refused him room. But the loneliness of Jesus, like much loneliness in the Bible and in the life of faith, must also be seen as the result of an active obedience and loyalty to God. God calls people to belong to him and so breaks them away from other belongings: "'Follow me', said Jesus, "and leave your father and mother and other belongings'" (Matt 10:34-39). Abram had to go out from his father's house, to be a wanderer in the desert, not knowing where he was going, in order to become the father of all the faithful (Rom 4:16-22).

This separation or breaking of belonging is not exclusively the terrible privilege of those who are called to be heroes of the faith or martyrs. It is in the texture of ordinary life. So it is natural and expected that a person will leave his father and mother in order to cleave to another. The foundation of healthy marriage is not merely belonging, but separation. Marriages sometimes break down because we do not know how to belong, sometimes because we do not know how to forsake all others.

Parenting is only good when it accepts the separation: even from its beginnings, parenting involves creating distance, not instead of love but as the form of respectful, hopeful love. Children do not belong to their parents. 'Belong' is a dangerous word because we associate it with property, with what we have at our disposal and indeed may dispose of, if we will. No one belongs to anyone else like that: slavery is wrong, despite the fact that in various forms it is still rampant in the world.

The first witness to Jesus the Risen One was told not hold on to him but to respect the separation involved in dying and returning to the Father (John 20:17).

Many of the wrongs that people do to each other arise not from a failure to belong but from the failure to respect and enable separation. People do not give others space to be themselves; we do not tolerate difference; we cannot live with the sense of loneliness and insecurity that comes with respecting the otherness of other people. So we do violence to people to satisfy our hunger for belonging. Accepting that rape is possible in marriage makes the point plain: even in this most committed belonging, there is no right of possession; rather respect for the separateness of the other is essential for the well-being and justice of the union. 'Belonging', being 'united', or 'together', is so often assumed to be unambiguously good that we need to explore the ways in which separation and difference also have to be valued and lived.

TO THINK ABOUT

Two missionaries called to Chile have two children aged 16 & 11. Their pastor says: "The Lord will look after them." Another friend says: "You must always put your family first."

What would you say?

Father, the hour has come (Jn 17:1)

Is the Church about preparation for separations or just about creating cosy belonging?

Conclusion

Churches want to build welcoming communities where people will feel at home. They work on people to bring them together and they even have worship in which God is 'invited' to come in and be welcome – as though God is not already there welcoming us.

Churches evoke a cosy intimacy which can obscure our primary belonging which involves separations. Churches are not good at preparing people for their primary calling to follow Christ which involves all the cost and challenge and loneliness mentioned above. We need to hold two elements in tension – both affirming and nurturing the strength, encouragement and support of belonging in Christian community, but also recognising that this is a means to a higher end – that of accomplishing the purposes of the Kingdom. Our religion is a shield from, rather than an exploration of, the separations which are part of our pilgrimage of life and death. When that happens the light of the gospel goes out in the church.

God is the great and faithful belonger. He chooses people and says: "You will be my People and I will be your God". He makes and upholds strong covenants. Yet God never diminishes the difference between God and humanity. It is precisely because he is different that he sustains the belonging: "I am God, not man, therefore I will not come to destroy" (Hosea 11:9).

FAMILY VALUES

WORKSHEET

1 *'In human communities people can experience God's grace ... too often, however, these communities and their institutions become substitutes for belonging to God.'*

List the 'institutions' and organisations you belong to. How does each help or hinder your sense of belonging to God?

Institution/organisation	Helps	Hinders	Not sure

2 What do you understand by 'traditional family values'?

What family values have most helpfully shaped your life?

3 Some people suggest that we should 'go back' to a time when family values were better and stronger.

● What aspects of family life in the past would you be happy to return to?

● What are you pleased to have left behind?

● Which period of history do you regard as being 'a golden age' for families and why?

4 What is your church doing to help families?

Belonging

5   *'The family is, and will continue to be, more a barometer of our troubles than an escape from them.'*

What do you understand by this phrase, and how do you think it should influence the way churches address problems in families?

6   Read John 1:11 and Rom 5:8-10. What do verses like these tell us about how Jesus created 'Christian belonging'?

• What are the implications for followers of Jesus if they are to create a 'belonging' for others?

7   *'Belonging is not found without wrestling with loneliness.'*

• Is the Bible as much about separations as about belongings (Matt 10:34-39; Rom 4:16-22; John 20:7)?

• List some of the 'separations' the Bible speaks of and others that are significant in your life or the lives of those around you.

• How does the church prepare people for the 'separations'?

8   What should the church be for people? (Tick the most appropriate boxes and then rank your choices in order of priority.)

Like a ...

☐ warm duvet, cosy and comforting   ☐ nourishing meal

☐ kick in the pants; challenging   ☐ big, happy family

☐ shot in the arm, stimulating   ☐ dangerous expedition

☐ other................................

....

....

> One practical thing I resolve to do as a result of this study is .....

Share your answers, and discuss whether your church is more concerned to create a good internal life than to enable people to live for God beyond the fellowship.

Belonging

Belonging &

COMMUNITY LIVING

The notion of an extended family is largely alien to contemporary Western culture. To the majority of people, the term 'family' immediately conjures up a two-generation nuclear family of parents and children. There are, however, some significant variations to this in British society. This chapter seeks to explore some alternative models of 'family' and encourages us to consider ways that community can be developed at all levels.

CHANGING PATTERNS IN SOCIETY

Family Size is Shrinking

Over 25% of households in 1991 consisted of one person living alone. This was almost double the proportion in 1961 and continues a trend since the Second World War.

Ethnic minority households tend to be the largest, with Bangladeshi families averaging five members. This is partially accounted for by three generations within the family unit.

In contemporary Western usage the minimum criterion for a family unit is one parent plus a child. In 1991 families headed by lone mothers and lone fathers amounted to 18% of all families with dependent children.

Isolation is Increasing

Current British government policy offers little if any incentives which encourage citizens to extend family and kinship groups in order to care for the elderly, weak and vulnerable members of society. Research has shown, however, that, for example, old people prefer to be cared for in the home rather than in state-run institutions. Yet even from a merely financial perspective, it makes more sense for the state to enable families to care for their members than to institutionalise them, unless their needs require specialist care.

These social trends, combined with government policy, put strain not only on individuals who are becoming increasingly isolated, but also on resources. Housing stock is put under further pressure by shrinking and dividing family units. More energy and consumer durables are used up, so environmental resources are depleted. Individualism is not good for people or the planet, nor is it God's plan for us.

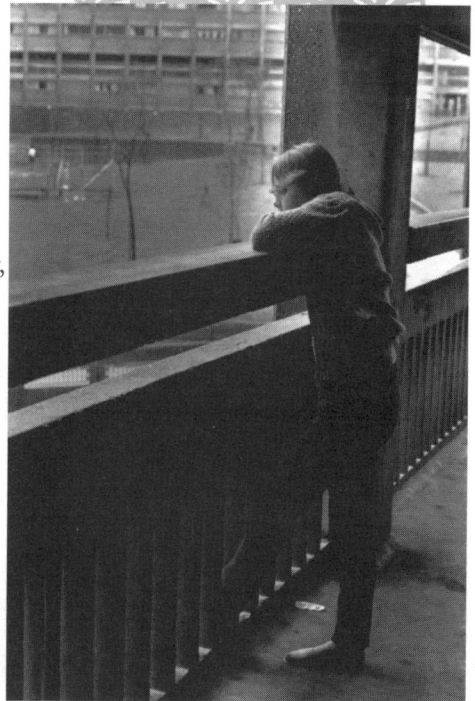

John Twinning

BIBLICAL PERSPECTIVES

In the Old and New Testaments there appear to be 'extended families' of two
models. One is based on kinship ties, the second is based on the response to
God's love and character, and his call to live out a set of alternative values within
society.

Old Testament

Kinship Links

By modern Western standards, the patriarchal family of Old Testament times was
a very large grouping. It included the father, mother(s), sons, daughters, brothers,
sisters (until marriage when they joined their husband's family), grandparents,
other kinsmen, as well as servants, concubines and needy people who had
appealed to the family for help. In Jacob's case we are told that 'he took with him
to Egypt his sons and grandsons and his daughters and granddaughters – all his
offspring' (Gen 46:7) and that all who went to Egypt with him, 'those who were
his direct descendants, not counting his sons' wives – numbered sixty-six persons'
(Gen 46:26).

Throughout the Old Testament period, the family was clearly one of the most
stable social structures in Israel. God's intention was that within the structure of
family people should learn to live in close relationships, caring for others and not
just for oneself; valuing people of all ages, status and background; practising a
lifestyle which involves interdependence rather than independence and removes
the dread of isolation.

The 'Family' Beyond

God also calls his people to extend their compassion beyond the kinship
group. The fast, says Isaiah, which is pleasing to God is not going through
the motions of a hollow ritual but displaying self-sacrificing compassion to
the hungry and poor – sharing food, providing shelter – and working in
costly ways for justice and freedom (Isa 58:6-10; cf Psa 68:6).

New Testament

Kinship Links

The New Testament similarly builds on the Old Testament model of kinship ties.
Jesus strongly condemns the Pharisees for encouraging any abdication of
responsibility to parents on seemingly religious grounds (Mk 7:11-13). Paul,
likewise, stresses the serious implications of failing to fulfil obligations towards
members of your family (1 Tim 5:8). The early church congregations were based
on 'family' households, which were able to absorb people as they had need. There
is an implicit affirmation of the wider extended family network.

The 'Family' Beyond

However, the New Testament takes our responsibility to the wider networks to
new levels.

Kinship links are no longer the only determining factor. Jesus introduces other
forms of family linkages – those based on a response to the call of God. At

various points Jesus seems to indicate that blood ties must come second to the demands of God (Matt 10:34-39; Lk 9:59-62) and to the needs of the family of faith (Lk 8:19-21; Matt 12:46-50; Mk 10:29-31).

Jesus calls people to a new model of community living, built on principles of mutual love and responsibility (Jn 15:12-13); simplicity in lifestyle (Mk 6:8-12); shared commitment to mission, prayer and worship (Lk 10:2-4; Matt 10:5-10). It is unlikely that he ever envisaged more than small local communities of believers who met in homes, and had an impact through their loving relationships and service to others.

The images Jesus uses of the Kingdom growing are based on believers acting as salt, light, yeast – quietly permeating and affecting wider society for the good (Lk 13:18-20). Believers are to be subversive in their activity, challenging the norms '…but I say to you …' (Matt 5:22, 28, 32, 39, 44).

This simplicity and shared community life is reflected in the early chapters of the Book of Acts (Acts 2:42-47 and 4:32-37). These reveal much social and financial interdependence, although clearly there were problems early on (Acts 5:1-11).

The very early Christians clearly believed in being alternative communities. Their faith affected their living – producing new sets of values, relationships and living patterns, and this had great impact on surrounding society (Acts 2:47).

THE CHURCH AND EXTENDED COMMUNITY

The biblical material presents us with models of family that are extended and with patterns of living as Christian communities that radically challenge much of our church life in contemporary Britain.

In an age when many in our society see the church as culturally irrelevant, is it not time to face the biblical challenges and risk developing new models of 'being church'? At present much of our energy and thinking is focused on the institution of the church. Perhaps we need to recover something of the spirit of the early Christians and refocus on our homes and weekday lives as the primary expressions of our faith, and ask searching questions as to how these witness to the Kingdom of God.

The present nuclear family that lives in its own little box and exhibits a lifestyle identical to its neighbours, except that it attends church on Sunday, does little to express the radical teaching of Jesus Christ.

Challenges to the Church

The challenge to extend our families
To offer hospitality and welcome to others, be they relatives, or any in need. To absorb the vulnerable into the relative safety and stability of Christian homes.

The challenge to share our resources
Deepening interdependence and a sense of community within the church community can be done by encouraging sharing of possessions and resources. Borrowing rather than buying is a way of resisting the prevailing values of materialism and consumerism.

This involves nurturing a sense of corporate stewardship rather than private ownership. Can we learn to view our resources as given for the benefit of all, and within small groups develop mutual accountability for the way we use our finances, time and gifts?

The challenge to recover our mission

The parables of Jesus lead us to ask significant questions about the ways in which we are permeating our society with the good news of the Kingdom. How many of our churches have a strategy to make their local communities happier, healthier, more whole places?

Advantages of Greater Community

1   A stronger sense of 'belonging' for more people, particularly those who do not find themselves in a nuclear family.

2   Potentially less stress – more members, for example, in a 'family' can share the burden of caring for a more vulnerable member.

3   Resources can be freed for other uses such as mission when people share more.

4   Greater inter-dependence exhibits deepened relationships and makes loving more real.

5   Greater sharing places less of a strain on the environment.

6   Simplifying our lifestyles witnesses to a set of alternative values that say people are more important than possessions.

7   A more community-centred lifestyle gives a more credible platform from which to challenge the forces in society that tend to alienate and oppress.

8   The message of the gospel has a greater credibility when backed by a more authentically 'gospel' lifestyle.

Tensions for the Church

Our desire for conformity

It is very human to want to be like everybody else and not to stand out from the crowd. Some Christians would argue that it is off-putting to outsiders to see Christians living too differently from them – it raises barriers. Others would say that Jesus called his followers to live in ways radically different from the norms of society, and that until the church exhibits some of these radical values, the integrity and life-transforming quality of the gospel is compromised. We need to face this tension and find ways to support each other in living differently.

Our desire for privacy

Many of us are grateful that we can close our doors on the world and escape into the safe haven of a place that is fully ours. More open households challenge this desire because the 'world' enters our space. Likewise we value emotional privacy; we are not keen on exposing our feelings, thinking and weaknesses to others. A deeper level of community is threatening because it makes us vulnerable, and because it demands more of us. We will have to deal with the pain as well as the pleasure of deeper relationships.

Our desire for comfort

A greater sharing of our resources with others inevitably means less for ourselves.

This may be difficult. We may feel that, whilst as adults we can cope with less, it is not fair to 'disadvantage' our children.

Our desire for security and institutional frameworks

Christianity became institutionalised very early in its life. We now live with the legacy that we 'go to church' rather than we 'are the church'. For many there is great security in the traditional frameworks of the past, and any attempt to challenge these deeply-cherished understandings and patterns of behaviour can meet with great resistance.

We have to realise that we are living in a post-Christendom era, and that the models of church life that served Christendom are no longer helpful today.

PRACTICAL INITIATIVES

Although major experiments in extended family or community living may be difficult for Christians to undertake in contemporary Western society, it is possible to take steps which extend both our understanding and practice of belonging. In opening our hearts and lives we may offer opportunities for others to experience that sense of belonging which is vital to every person's development and well-being.

Occasional Hospitality

For some it may be possible to offer hospitality on an occasional basis. Providing meals, friendship and a place of welcome and care is a vital ministry, much appreciated by many within the community.

- People moving into your area
- Students living away from home
- Foreign students settling into a new country
- People living on their own
- Fellow believers who are travelling reps
- Young homeless people – eg, through a Nightstop Scheme

Short-term Guests

Many opportunities exist for Christians to offer hospitality and extend a family environment to people needing loving care or practical support for a few weeks or months.

- People needing a break from dependent relatives
- The dependent relatives of the above
- People who need temporary refuge – eg, those who need protection and space to withdraw from a crisis situation, perhaps having been abused or involved in marriage breakdowns
- Children of friends who need a break from parenting responsibilities
- A child whose parent is in hospital
- Missionaries on furlough or home assignment
- People facing illness alone
- Patients needing post-operative care

Specialist Care

Some appropriately trained and equipped Christians may extend their family life by opening their homes to people in society who need specialist support and care.

- Children who require foster homes
- Children waiting to be adopted
- People coming off drugs and alcohol who need a half-way house
- Ex-prisoners needing a half-way home on the way to life fully back in society
- Residents in psychiatric institutions who would benefit from an experience of being in family and enjoy a sense of belonging

Steps Towards Community

Shared Ownership

Where people live near each other resources such as cars, washing machines and lawn mowers could be shared.

Where people are more widely scattered some churches have developed a tool bank. This can be for any items, but primarily for those that are not used frequently – power tools, decorating equipment, tile cutters, garden tools, sanders. People contribute the items they have, and then can 'hire' items out for a nominal charge. This money accrues and acts as a replacement or repair fund. The tool bank can also become a collection point for old or redundant tools that can be used by *Tools With a Mission* (sponsored by the Baptist Men's Movement) or other agencies that refit equipment for less-developed countries.

Still waiting for the community lawn-mower, then?

Corporate Buying

Groups of individuals can combine forces and buy in bulk in order to save money and packaging expenses.

The Battersea Wholefood Co-operative *Common Pulse* is an example of a scheme originally set up by Northcote Road Baptist Church in Battersea. Church members had order forms and would place an order once a month. A rota of people fetched the mainly fair-traded food from a warehouse in north London, and others weighed and bagged-up the bulk quantities. Prices included a margin that was used to fund development projects overseas.

The scheme gradually widened, and was an excellent contact point with many other non-church people in the neighbourhood.

Barter Economies

LOCAL TRADING SCHEMES WITH THEIR OWN CURRENCIES ARE SWEEPING THE COUNTRY *Guardian March 12th 1994.*

Bath has its 'olivers', Manchester – bobbins, Totnes – acorns, Southampton – solents and many more. Basically people offer their skills to each other – whether it is baking, ironing, cabinet making, decorating or legal advice – and accounts are debited or credited in the local currency. Siobhan Harper is one of 330 people in one of the largest local exchange trading schemes (or LETS) in the country:

"People feel this loss of neighbourliness. LETS gives them a tangible way to be neighbourly. It's a way of getting to know people, but it's not just a social circle. People are trading skills and resources so there's a productive positive relationship."

Could one run a similar system based on skill exchange amongst neighbouring churches – the local currency could be 'pews'.

More Developed Sense of Community

Communities that enable ministry

Chelmsley Wood, a church on a large urban estate in Birmingham, now has ministry thanks to the vision of a small group of friends who shared a commitment to facilitate ministry in a more difficult social area. A group supported one of their members to train for ministry. He teamed up with another minister at college, and now the four wage-earners in the group of six support the two ministers to work in the church. Sharing accommodation, finances and vision have freed resources that have enabled ministry in a community which otherwise could not have afforded it.

Communities that encourage an alternative spirituality

Nether Springs is the mother house for the Northumbrian community which is made up of people principally in Northumbria but scattered throughout Britain and as far afield as eastern Europe, Turkey and America. People come from all denominations and none. They are bound by a concern to see the Kingdom of God extended, and by a desire to explore the richness of a new kind of monasticism. The community upholds a Common Rule which is based on the two tenets of Availability and Vulnerability. These principles include commitment to prayer, hospitality, scripture and costly discipleship. They also share a common liturgy. The Northumbria community is based on a rediscovery of Celtic Spirituality, which emphasises a contemplative community fully incarnate in the realities of secular society, and expressing an alternative set of values and a 'fearful hope'.

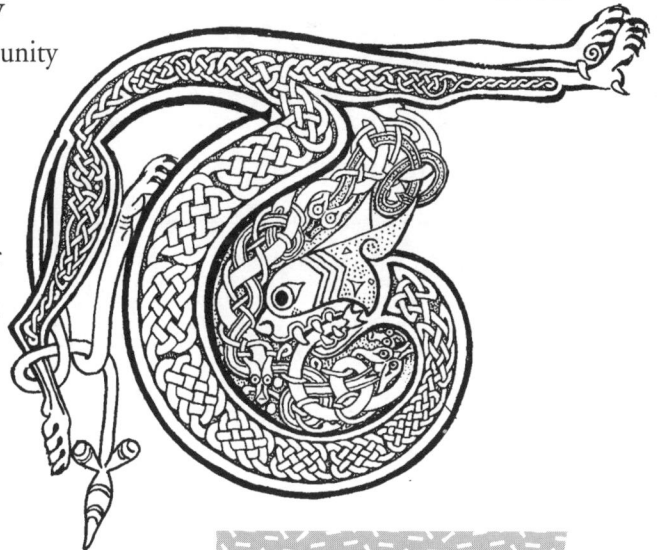

> ...AS THE LARK SAYS IN HER SONG;
> OFTEN, OFTEN, OFTEN, GOES CHRIST IN
> THE STRANGER'S GUISE.

39

1 Ian and Clare were discussing the fact that Carol and Derek's 83 year old mother had just been moved into an old people's home. (Carol and Derek are their friends at church and have three children: 8, 12 and 14 years.)

How would you have contributed to this discussion? Who is right?

Ian	*It's awful, they just ought to take Carol's mum into their home. We shouldn't just push responsibility onto the welfare state and expect others to do the dirty work.*
Clare:	*Be fair! There's not much room in their house, the children are still young and Carol works part-time. Her mum's only a couple of hours away; they can visit her at any time.*
Ian:	*Families should stick together. The state makes it all too easy for ties to loosen. Look at Joan and Ted – maybe if there wasn't so much state provision for single parents and the like, they'd have worked harder at keeping their marriage going.*
Clare:	*That's ridiculous! Surely we should support a society that cares for the vulnerable. It's not always possible or 'right' to put additional pressures on families.*
Ian:	*I'm not sure; as Christians we have a duty to the wider family. I read something the other day about Germany: they stopped providing state day-centres, and people have responded by forming networks of relationships that still enable care to be offered so that women can go to work. They seem to have put a new value on extended families because state help has been withdrawn.*
Clare:	*Good, well I'm glad you're so keen on the extended family. My mum and dad are having their house decorated and want to come and stay a few weeks …*
Ian:	*(gulp!)*

2 Family size is shrinking in the UK: eg, 25% of households in 1991 were occupied by one person living alone. What are the advantages and disadvantages of this?

Advantages	Disadvantages

3 If you did extend your family, what difficulties might other people have if they lived a closer community life with you?

● What strengths and resources could you offer to others if you lived a closer community life with them?

Belonging

4 Read Isaiah 58 (especially verses 6-9) and Matthew 25:34-40.

How do you, or how could you, fulfil the obligations that God lays before his people?

List responsibilities mentioned in text	Response as individuals	Response as a family group	Response as a Christian community

5 The Holy Spirit at Pentecost had a radical impact on the early disciples, not least in the area of how they viewed their property and possessions.

Read Acts 2:42-47 and Acts 4:32-37.

List on a central piece of paper the changes mentioned in these verses.

● What motivated the people to pool their resources?

● If we are challenged by their response, why do we find it so hard today to live out anything like this model?

6 What practical steps could you take that would increase the degree of sharing, interdependence and community within your fellowship?

Put these on a central piece of paper (and retain for a future church meeting!)

7 List some of these steps below and indicate your strength of feeling about them on a scale of 1-5; both those feelings which drive you to explore ways of strengthening community life and those which cause you to draw back from it.

Practical steps	Positive feelings					Negative feelings				
	5	4	3	2	1	1	2	3	4	5
eg: *Sharing Cars*				⟶		⟵				

● Which steps have least resistance to them?

● When do you start implementing them?

One practical thing I resolve to do
as a result of this study is .....

Belonging

Belonging &
SINGLENESS

Churches dare not ignore the large proportion of Britain's population who live alone: single, never married, divorced or separated, widowed. This chapter aims to encourage a greater understanding of single people and to explore ways of enhancing their sense of belonging, particularly within the church.

CHANGING PATTERNS IN SOCIETY

There are more single adults in Western society and in the church than ever before. In the UK, out of 46 million people over 16, nearly 17 million are single – that's 36%. (HMSO Statistics, 1992.)

Yet the church's constant emphasis is so much on family and marriage that it is in danger of marginalising this growing section of society.

So why are there so many more single adults? George Bernard Shaw's dictum is no longer true:

> it is a woman's business to get married as soon as possible, and a man's to keep unmarried as long as he can.

The age of marrying is going up for both women and men and fewer adults now get married, some choosing to cohabit. (Government figures for 1992 showed 2.3 million cohabiting adults – 18% of all unmarried people aged 16-59.)

There are other contributory trends:

- More marriages are ending in divorce or separation, fewer divorcees are remarrying.
- The number of lone parents is growing: a few from choice, most by necessity, but totalling 21% of all families, which is the highest national proportion anywhere in the world.
- Better health care means that widows and widowers are living longer.
- The homosexual community is possibly growing, although reliable statistics are hard to come by.

But there are some deeper, albeit more disputable, issues. Selfishness and affluence often go hand in hand. So a number of single people simply enjoy the ability to live on their own, in comfort and total self-centredness. If that basic selfishness is not addressed, then the chances are that any marriage will end in disaster.

Within most Baptist churches, singles are a significant group. The Evangelical Alliance survey in 1992 found that about 35% of adults in churches were single; only a little less than the national figure for the whole population. Despite popular myths, the proportions of single women and single men under 30 in church are about the same. However, in Baptist churches the imbalance of single women to single men over the age of 45 is very pronounced at 70:30.

I used to introduce myself as a "childless, single-parent family", just to get in on the act.

'Singles-blindness' is a feature of much church life, because, although such a large group, single people are often 'hidden', representing as they do, such a diversity within the church community: young and old, unmarried, divorced, widowed… It is a helpful and often revealing exercise to work out the percentage of single adults in your congregation.

▶ Identify the single people in your church as a proportion of the total membership.

BIBLICAL PERSPECTIVES

God created male and female in his image, to live together, for it was not good for either of them to be alone. Yet when God became human, he chose an unmarried woman to be his mother, and then chose a life of celibacy till his death. And this illustrates the ambiguity with which the Bible treats singleness; and indeed the ambiguity with which the historic churches have viewed the subject: single priests, monks and nuns, exhorting and protecting family values.

The Genesis story makes it clear that the complementary union of male and female is at the heart of the fight against loneliness and isolation. Paul points to the mystical paradigm in the sexual union, representing Christ and his Bride, the Church. In fact, both Old and New Testaments are full of sexual imagery, illustrating the closeness of God to his people, or the idolatry of 'playing the harlot' with foreign gods. Humans are made in the image of God, and our sexuality perhaps reflects the eternal intimacy within the Godhead. This is why our sexuality and spirituality are so closely connected. Consider this definition: 'longing for intimacy, to know and be known, desiring to comprehend the other and be totally comprehended by them; to love and be loved, to be fully at one with, absorbed by and absorbing the loved one.' This could be a partial definition of human sexual union, or Christian spirituality.

▶ Do you find this close link between sexuality and spirituality either helpful or unhelpful in understanding your relationship with God, and why?

Part of the answer lies in Genesis 3, where the Fall clearly disrupts the male/female relationship as well as the humanity/God relationship. It is at this time also that there is a distortion in one of God's greatest gifts, human sexuality. Marriage can never be the same again, and arguably, neither is it to be the sole solution for loneliness. There is an 'aloneness' which drives a person to God, and which even marriage cannot alleviate. And there is a closeness to God through the Second Adam, which Adam and Eve never knew.

> *For a member of the Body of Christ, marriage is no longer a necessity or duty, for man is no longer alone as Adam was; he is the friend of Christ, he lives in the communion of saints, and he is indwelt by the Holy Spirit.*
>
> Max Thurian

In 1Corinthians 7, Paul speaks of singleness, either for a period, or for life, as:

a gift for the individual (v7). It is no use the person saying they do not have 'the gift'. For as long as they are single, then they have the gift and have to make the most of it. Of course, they can work hard at trying to exchange the gift for that of marriage if they so choose – this may mean changing church, or at least making sure they are in places where they are likely to meet suitable spouses.

a gift for the Church (vv 17, 28-33). Down through the centuries, the Church has benefited enormously from men and women who have had the freedom and

TO THINK ABOUT:

If sexual union appears to be an integral part of our human image-of-God-ness, why does Paul extol singleness as the 'better way', and why was the only totally fulfilled human unmarried?

lack of ties to serve God in special and sometimes courageous ways. And until recently, single Christians were regarded by the church as special blessings from God. Only over the last century or so has the Protestant church begun to pity and ostracise them. If 35% of your church is single, what proportion of the leadership is single?

a gift for the Lord (v 35), displaying 'undivided devotion'. This may have reflected Paul's own experience, and certainly there is plenty of evidence in the writings of single men and women down through church history who have had a 'special' closeness to Christ. (Francis of Assisi, Lady Julian of Norwich, Abbess Hildegarde, David Brainerd…)

Christ also extols singleness in a short but revolutionary (for the Jews) little addendum to a pathetic remark by the disciples after his teaching on divorce (Matt 19:1-12). His three categories of 'eunuchs' may represent:

(i) those physically or psychologically unable to consummate marriage – there are many with 'wounds' from the past or a sexual orientation that makes them choose not to marry;

(ii) victims of circumstance – divorce, the death of a spouse, obligation to care for parents or family, or just being in a place where there are no suitable partners;

(iii) those who choose, for a period, or for life, not to marry – or remarry.

> Marriage and singleness are different today than in Paul's day. How do you think the passages apply to us?
>
> Are there things that only single people can achieve in the church? Are there things only married people can achieve?

THE CHURCH AND SINGLENESS

There is no doubt that for many single people their biggest problem is the rest of the church. Most churches just don't take single adults seriously. They are a negative by-product of failure to find a partner, failure to hold on to a partner and make a marriage work, or failure to die at the same time as their partner. The well-meaning comments at weddings, "your turn next!", the concerned conversations, "and she's such a nice girl…", the assumption that if you are a leader you are married, and the obvious confusion when they discover you are not, "Oh, I'm sorry… ". These can all contribute to a sense of failure and of exclusion. It is the steady dripping of a tap that exacerbates the feeling of isolation and unfulfilled longing which is both the privilege and pain of the single life.

Even preachers sometimes illustrate their sermons as if the entire world is married and has children. And then suddenly remembering the singles they throw in a "some of you will find out about that soon enough… ".

There is a common assumption that those who have never been married 'can't understand', which presumably means that Jesus is not able to sympathise with married people.

As in so many other areas, there is also a gender bias here against women. The word 'bachelor' has overtones of freedom and choice; 'spinster' smacks of hair in a bun and sensible shoes. Men are allowed to keep their options open into their mid thirties, although beyond that they must be immature and there must also be some suspicion about their sexual orientation. Women, however, are pitiable from the late twenties onwards. Their biological clock is ticking away, and

although men in their fifties may marry a younger woman and have a family, the reverse is rarely witnessed or possible.

But single people are sometimes their own worst enemies. They too must shoulder some of the blame for isolation. For they must guard against a self-centredness which wants the benefits of extended family with none of the down side – children and chores must be part of the self-giving which integrates us into society. And there is nothing worse than the single person who simply wants an audience to listen attentively to their tale of woe and bitter recriminations against the lot that life has landed them.

There are also those who cut off their noses to spite their faces! They won't ring anyone, write or visit, and interpret lack of contact by their friends as a sign of lack of love and concern. Sometimes it is indeed thoughtlessness on their friends' part, but more often it is the busyness of normal family life. Single people must pursue friendships in a way that marrieds often need not. Then again, what a sense of belonging I experience when someone from a busy family rings me 'just to see that I'm OK'.

Celibacy

Until quite recently in the protestant tradition, celibacy was encouraged as a real option, either for the early years, or for life. This was the apostle Paul's attitude. But very rarely nowadays is celibacy regarded as a way of serving the Lord wholeheartedly. Rather it is regarded as an odd quirk, tolerated more in older people (who are 'past it') than in younger people, and of course, in female missionaries. I am generally worried by people who say, "I don't want to be married. I'm perfectly happy being single." But I am encouraged when I meet those who explain, "Yes, I would like to be married. But I have chosen to be single for the present." We should encourage people to explore celibacy as a calling from God. They don't necessarily have to take any 'vows', but they can know the liberty of being free from the continual search for a partner.

> *When I was in my twenties and early thirties, I was fully expecting to marry, but when the moment of decision came I lacked assurance that this was God's will, and so drew back. I began to ask myself at that time whether God was calling me to be single. I have never had a revelation from God. I have never taken vows of celibacy. It's been the force of circumstances.*
>
> John Stott

> *I believe God has a need and purpose for some of us to be single and so available where others cannot be; He has some works for which a woman's nature and gifts are essential and that may mean that that woman cannot be shared with a husband and family. But He is not insensitive to the cost involved nor shocked by our questioning.*
>
> Hester Dain

Sexuality

Although sex is not usually the biggest problem for single people, the pressures in our society to be sexually active produce a real tension in this area. Arguably, this is no greater than the sexual tensions experienced by many married people. In my pastoral work I often find that single people have a better understanding of their sexuality – and other people's – than marrieds. This pressure is not dealt with by a denial of our sexual drive, but rather by a channelling of some of the sexual energy. 'The essence of chastity is not the suppression of lust but the total orientation of one's life toward a goal' (Dietrich Bonhoeffer). Orgasm therefore has to be ignored or, as some would allow, coped with through masturbation.

The longing for intimacy however, has to be addressed by community and friendship. So Jesus had his wider circle of friends: women, men, families. Then there were his daily companions: the twelve disciples. But he had his three best friends: Peter, James and John; and of them, John was his intimate 'beloved' friend. Sadly, few churches would tolerate such favouritism either amongst married or unmarried leaders. (And the disciples found it pretty hard to stomach!)

But if Jesus, God incarnate, needed such companionship and physical touch, then we must recognise that singles in order to survive need degrees of physical and mental intimacy with others. Hug someone who is widowed this Sunday! The degrees of intimacy will vary with personality, culture, age and many other factors. But for singles to feel that their 'singleness' is accepted, and that they truly belong, the noble gift of intimate friendship must be revived. This will make some feel a little uncomfortable. But then David and Jonathan or Jesus and John have always made a few feel uncomfortable. There is little teaching in many of our churches on 'soul friends' and companionship.

Jesus took children in his arms, and it is still children who will often provide, without the self-conscious embarrassment experienced by most British adults, the affection and acceptance which the single person needs. To hold a baby in your arms and give it it's 'bottle', can be a deeply affirming experience for a single person.

> Recall some recent occasions when some physical contact, some gesture of affection, understanding or affirmation encouraged you.
>
> What reasons either make you comfortable or uncomfortable in expressing your feelings towards others through touch.
>
> What would you want to see changed in the teaching of your church, to help include single people more fully?
>
> What pastoral work would you like to see to help single people with identity and self-acceptance; relationships and sexuality; social pressures?

PRACTICAL INITIATIVES

How can the church release the potential of single people and help them, with all God's people, to become mature in Christ? And how can the church be a community which reaches out to help the 36% of our population who are single? The ideas below are equally applicable to people within the church family, and as importantly, to those who live alone in wider community.

Extended Families

Extended families are a great gift, although they sometimes stretch the boundaries of our selfless love and tolerance. Simply to be 'included in' on family life, at weekends and at Christmas, on shopping trips or helping with

Dad! Dad! We've forgotten Uncle Ray!

children's birthday parties, on holidays or painting the kitchen (yours or theirs!); all these are ways of reinforcing among the unmarried, widows and widowers, sole parents, their sense of belonging. It must not become abuse or exploitation. Many marrieds wrongly assume that single people have all the time in the world for running everything in the church, as well as baby-sitting. Extended families must operate out of genuine friendship, mutuality, help and support, not out of pity. Worse still, some married couples almost flaunt the success of their relationship before singles. Conversely, what a sense of belonging I had when my first 'extended family' gave me a key to their door!

Lone Parents

Lone parents have particular needs of acceptance and space. To be free occasionally from the constant demands of their children is a great boon. And their children may lack a father or mother role model. Secure couples, especially older ones whose children may have flown the nest, may consider sharing their house with such lone parents. Some churches have enabled two or more lone parents to buy or rent property together so that parenting and household work can be shared. A creche or child-minding service can be of enormous service to those within and outside of the immediate church community. (See the Parenting section for more ideas p73.)

Widows and Widowers

Arranging sometimes for widows and widowers to meet, specifically to talk about bereavement and adjusting to single life again may be a practical service. Many 'put on a brave face' while inside they are hurting and longing to talk about the pain of separation, and the aloneness they feel so acutely. It doesn't go away after a year or so when the rest of the fellowship have got used to the new lone partner. This is another opportunity to reach out into the needy unchurched community. Sometimes social services will put a church in touch with those not coping with bereavement.

> *The assertion made by a happy marriage often alienates, and is at least half consciously intended to alienate, the excluded spectator.*
>
> Iris Murdoch

The Basingstoke Community Church is a well-known New Church with 200 single people. Single people are fully integrated into the life and ministry of the fellowship which includes a Christian school and a Pregnancy Crisis Centre.

They recently held a 12 week series on issues affecting singles. The programme was planned by 12 single people of different ages and between 70-100 attended each week. Discussions and testimonies surrounded the message.

Dave Richards writes: *The ministry was excellent. The discussions were not always easy because of the age range (16-75 years) but soon each grouping began to appreciate each other…*
… and where did we take what we had learned in these teaching sessions? Back to the local church where it all belongs. There are not special 'singles Sundays', no 'Statutory Single on everything', but a renewed hope that we would each discover our place and minister faithfully in it.

Taken from: *One of Us,* by Steve Chilcraft

Other Ideas

There are many simple ways of helping. I am always grateful for those who invite me to share their Sunday lunch, or to have supper with them on a lonely Sunday night. I am not too well-pleased, however, if I find they have also invited, without telling me, someone whom they think would make a perfect partner for me. Matchmaking has its place, but it must be done discreetly, and never forced. And I will offer to come round and cook a meal for the family sometimes, or invite them out to a restaurant if I can afford it, or turn up with a takeaway, or just take the kids to MacDonalds...

In sum, both marrieds and singles must work hard at accepting one another, giving a sense of belonging, fostering security and trusting love. Marrieds should let single people enjoy their singleness, and help save them from any encroaching bitterness. Don't patronise or pity, but receive from them and offer to them, remembering that you started out 'single' and that you may well end this life 'single'. And singles must make the most of the particular freedoms and opportunities which God has given them–- for as long as they last.

Recommendations of the EA Consultation on Singleness

In all the following recommendations we recognise the responsibility of single people to contribute to all aspects of church life.

1   The church needs to develop a theology of singleness within the context of a biblical understanding of relationships within the Kingdom.

2   We need to recognise the calling of single people to take their equal place within local and national church leadership.

3   By teaching, example and support, those working with youth should present celibacy as a positive and fulfilling way of life.

4   We need to recover a biblical emphasis on the spiritual gift of celibacy and find positive ways of presenting this to the church and the world.

5   Opportunities for exploring alternative models of community living should be provided. Economic pressure acting against this, particularly for younger single people, must be tackled, eg, through new methods of housing provision.

6   Churches should aim to foster a depth of relationship amongst their members and avoid either isolating single people or pressuring them into marriage. This may include what some understand as 'covenant' commitment.

7   Churches should be encouraged to give a greater level of practical pastoral support to single people going through major changes in their lives, and those caring for adult dependents.

8   There is a need for retirement preparation appropriate for single people and positive channelling of their gifts into a continuing ministry.

9   Churches should recognise and involve themselves in the housing needs of elderly single people.

10   Churches should actively seek to integrate single parents, separated, divorced and widowed people into the church community, eg, through hospitality, corporate social activities, shared discipleship groups.

11   Churches should take every opportunity to grow in awareness of the practical needs of single parents and their children and give appropriate support, eg, child care, house maintenance, family link schemes.

12   Churches should seek to provide for emotional healing, through prayer and counselling, for those whose identity and relationships have suffered damage.

13   Churches should establish relevant evangelistic structures directed towards the needs of single people and give active support to those engaged in evangelism and care amongst them.

14   Forums within churches should be created for single and married people together to discuss personal issues of sexuality.

15   Radical rethinking is required of the concept and practice of 'family' services.

16   Preachers should remember that their congregations include people leading single lifestyles.

17   In church decision-making and government, greater consideration should be given to the perspective of the whole range of single members of the congregation.

18   Increased efforts should be made to recognise, develop and direct the gifts of all single people.

19   Shared holidays between married couples and single people could be encouraged.

20   Existing pastoral structures should be assessed and restructured as necessary in the light of the needs of single people.

▶   **At what occasion(s) might these recommedations be considered by your church?**

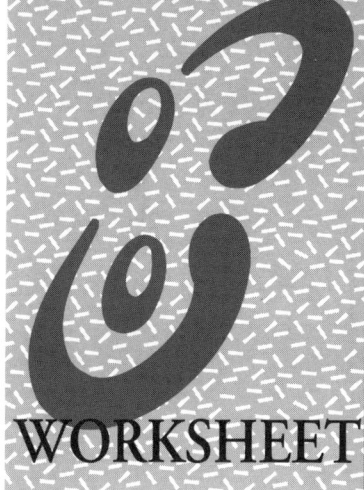

Notes to leaders

You will need copies of your church address list, if available, and to have done the preparatory work mentioned in question 1. You will also need Bibles.

1 Obtain copies of your church list, enough for one for every 2-3 in the group. Count up those in the congregation never-married, divorced, separated and widowed and fill in the box below. (NB a leader could save time by working out the total beforehand and supplying a calculator.)

- What surprises you about the figures?

	Never Married	Divorced/ Separated	Widowed	Proportion of Single People to Total
Male				
Female				
Total				

2 Do single people feel at home in the social life of your church? If not, why not?

- What are some of the attitudes and comments one hears expressed about single people?

3 Read 1 Corinthians 7:32-34 and Ephesians 5:21-33.

- What are these passages saying about singleness?

- Marriage and singleness are different today than in Paul's day. How do you think the passages apply to us?

- What contributions may only single people bring to a church?

4 Overheard at the church door – *In the Cultural Revolution in China, young people had to remain single until the age of 28 in order to serve the state. The church should have an equivalent scheme: temporary voluntary singleness in order to give time and energy to Christian service.*
How do you respond to that point of view?

5 Several scenarios are outlined overleaf. In small groups of 2-3 select two and try to answer the following questions. (NB: It doesn't matter if groups are studying the same scenario.)

- How has the church been helpful in this situation?
- How could the church have been more sensitive and caring?
- How would your church cope with this particular scenario?

Belonging

Liz is in her late twenties and lives in a small community. Her job entails some travel and she can be away from home for several days every week. This makes it difficult for her to get involved with her church fellowship. Much of her social contact is with her working colleagues, none of whom are Christians although they are of a similar age. One in particular has asked her out on several occasions and she is struggling with the reasons given for not going out with non-Christians (2 Cor 6:14). How would you advise her? What steps may she need to take?

Steve has struggled for many years with the knowledge that he has a strong homosexual orientation. As a committed Christian he knows that the practice of homosexuality is not an option for him. However, he does not find women physically attractive and so the only apparent option is celibacy. Steve is ashamed to admit his homosexual orientation amongst Christian friends, due to violent reactions during discussions on the subject. Consequently he admits only to "not having met the right girl" and is thus the victim of matchmaking attempts, a source of great embarrassment.

Harry was widowed at the age of 55. Gradually he began attending church, encouraged by the minister who had comforted him during his wife's long illness. Having made a Christian commitment, he has become increasingly involved in the life of the church and community. He is also actively involved in visiting and cooking for the sick, and travels abroad regularly. Harry has a wide and ever increasing circle of friends and enjoys life immensely.

A young lesbian woman, who has been a Christian for a few years and is living a celibate life, opens up to her housegroup leader that she is lonely and frustrated. She is reluctant to tell the whole church because she doesn't know how they would react. She feels she needs friends and more people around her as she lives on her own. She wonders whether she should tell the rest of the housegroup so that they can be aware of her situation. However, the leader is worried about one or two housegroup members' ability to keep confidentialities and the attitude of one member towards homosexuality. How should the housegroup leader react? What support structures should be brought in to support this young woman? How can she be made to feel included instead of excluded?

Dave and Angela work in the same office. Both are in their mid thirties and both hold very responsible jobs. They are involved separately in many aspects of Christian service within their local churches. Both are fulfilled in their work and whilst feeling lonely on occasions they have no desire to "marry for the sake of it". They have a good friendship and have been a source of encouragement and companionship to each other, though there is no romantic involvement at all. Sadly, it is almost impossible for them to maintain a normal friendship due to constant pressure from friends who have decided that they are perfect for each other. Consequently they have chosen not to see each other socially simply for a "quiet life".

● Compare your findings with the rest of the groups.

6 What would you want to see changed in the teaching of your church to help include single people more fully?

● What pastoral work would you like to see to help single people with questions of identity, self-acceptance, relationships, sexuality and social pressures?

One practical thing I resolve to do as a result of this study is .....

7 What could your church offer to single people in the wider community?

Belonging

MARRIAGE

This chapter examines the current social scene and the biblical material on marriage and then explores practical initiatives which churches could take to prepare couples for marriage, enrich marriages and offer support to those under stress.

CHANGING PATTERNS IN SOCIETY

'Love, love changes everything' states the theme song from Andrew Lloyd Webber's musical *Aspects of Love* . Society as a whole has this mistaken wishful thinking at the heart of what has become known as the sexual revolution. The following statistics throw some light on the current attitudes to marriage.

- 90% of people in the U.K. will be married for a part of their lives.

Marriage on the Decline

However, the number of marriages is declining.
- In 1991 only 55% of households were headed by a married couple and by the year 2000 this figure is likely to fall below 50%.
- In a third of all marriages in 1991 one or both partners had been divorced.

Cohabitation on the Increase

Cohabitation is becoming increasingly common among both single and divorced or separated men and women. Most people who cohabit do so with one partner only, and subsequently enter into a marriage relationship with that person. Most periods of cohabitation are short, being less than two years, and are most usually a stage leading to marriage.

- A survey conducted by the Marriage and Partnership Research Unit of the Central Middlesex Hospital predicts that by the year 2000 80% of couples will have cohabited before marriage.
- Figures produced by the Anglican parishes in London reveal that in 1993 up to 90% of couples seeking marriage were living together.

We are living in the midst of a sexual revolution brought about by advances in medicine; changes in society's attitudes and teaching; economic pressures (eg, cost of housing); and the influence of a high divorce rate.

Those whom we speak to will talk of love-filled sex, as either an anticipation of marriage, or a trial marriage, or they will reject any need of a religious ceremony in their relationship.

In 1992 nearly 1 in 5 unmarried people aged 16-59 were cohabiting.

People co-habiting as a proportion of the unmarried population

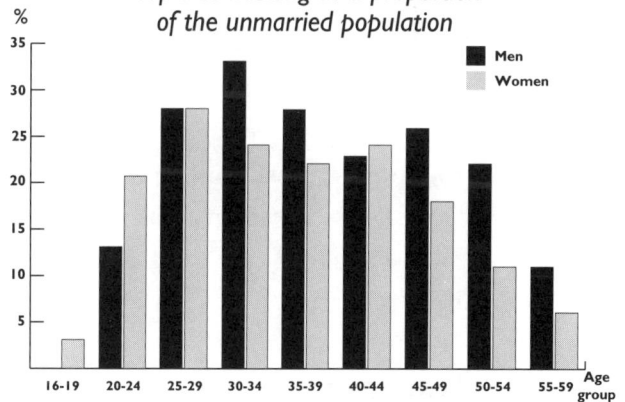

Given the statistics that couples are older before they marry (24 for women, 26 for men) how realistic is it to insist that such couples do not sleep together prior to marriage? What is the effect of the church promoting this view strongly?

BIBLICAL PERSPECTIVES

Biblical teaching is clear and direct, but it doesn't say quite what we expect it to say. The church has generally got a bad press when it comes to human sexuality, usually being seen as against it. We will need to recapture a biblical understanding of sexuality both inside and outside marriage, and present the biblical ideal of marriage to the church and an apologetic for marriage to the world. We will need to ask, when is a relationship a marriage? While English law says that there must be a wedding ceremony of some kind, we will need to ask questions about the inner workings of a relationship, and, in all honesty, admit that some cohabiting relationships are better than some marriages.

The Biblical Context

It is important to recognise the social context in which the Bible's teaching on marriage takes place. In Jewish society a woman had no other career than marriage, and she would normally marry at 12-14 years of age. Engagement would often take place in infancy. Betrothal was by dowry and legal document, and cohabitation often followed betrothal, although this was not approved of. Finally the wedding took place with a feast but no ceremony. Polygamy was legal and divorce relatively easy.

Don't they make a lovely couple?

In the Greek world a dowry was the legal cementing of a marriage, followed by the wedding which comprised five religious ceremonies. Again divorce was easy and common.

The Roman practice consisted of a two-stage process – the betrothal with the giving of a ring, a dowry and a legal promise, and then a religious ceremony. A civil contract was also available and common-law marriage through cohabitation was permissible.

Christianity confronted the lax morals and easy divorce within these three systems with teaching on separation, new life, new home, union, becoming one, reciprocity, partnership, and these for the whole of life. But the early church did not hold a religious ceremony, maybe recognising that a commitment to marriage was within the New Covenant Community (cf Paul's teaching in 1 Corinthians 6&7).

Old Testament

The foundation for our understanding of marriage is found in the opening chapters of Genesis. Genesis 1:26-27, 31 presents the goodness of creation, which is underlined in Song of Songs 4:1-5; 5:10-16. Genesis 2:18-25 presents the relatedness and oneness of human sexuality, and Genesis 2:7 shows the interdependence and mutuality of male and female. Genesis 2:24 demonstrates that the covenant fidelity of one flesh relatedness comes before procreation. This wholeness leaves them naked and unashamed, and we see that unashamed eroticism is a feature of human sexuality before the Fall. The Song of Songs gives us the true picture of sexuality in relationship, while Genesis 3 paints a

> **What are the implications of this 'unashamed eroticism' for the Christian enjoyment of sexual intimacy?**

picture of a fall from God's purpose. The opening chapters of Hosea present the imagery of a faithful and forgiving marriage bond.

Gospels

In Christ we affirm our full sexuality; love's intensity, restraint, mutuality and permanence. We recognise Jesus' teaching that lust creates bad sex (Matt 5:28), leading from fantasy to destructive acts, and a denial of relationship. Jesus declares the pre-Fall design of God for committed relationships, affirming the life-unity of one flesh (Matt 19:4-6). Yet we must not lose sight of Jesus' attitude towards those in a cohabiting or adulterous relationship (Jn 4:16-26; 8:1-11); they are neither rejected nor condemned, but rather invited to find something new in Christ.

Epistles

In Paul's letter to the Ephesian church (5:21-33) the one flesh of marriage is worked out in mutual submission, sacrifice and love. The high-water mark of marriage relationship is compared to that of Christ and his Church (5:32), while in 1 Corinthians 7:3 Paul counsels mutual self-fulfilment within marriage. Human marriage is seen as God's purpose and a reflection of God's love. Sexual intercourse is reserved for the 'one flesh' of the marriage covenant (Gen 2:24 cf. Matt 19:6; Eph 5:28; 1 Cor 6:16).

The Bible speaks of God as love (1 John 4:8) and presents this sacrificial, self-giving, self-denying, faithful love as the basis of human relationships. It is this love that exists between husband and wife, it is the love of the crucified Christ for his church (Eph 5:21-33). Such love exists within the permanent covenant relationship that is marriage (Matt 19:8-9). The vows that form a part of the marriage service express the commitment and faithfulness of this covenant. In the Bible marriage is more than a private contract, it involves families and occurs within the context of the covenant community of the people of God. The community pledge their support to the couple.

> ▶ How does your church live out its pledge to support married couples?

THE CHURCH AND MARRIAGE

At a time when two in three marriages entered into in 1994 are likely to end in divorce and four out of five experience difficulties, and when marriages following cohabitation and second marriages are 60% more likely to fail than first marriages, there is a desperate need for the church to face up to its responsibility for supporting marriages. There is a need for us to recognise the situation, to face up to the whole area of human sexuality both outside and within marriage, and to engage in careful preparation for marriage. We will need to stress that premarital sex is privilege without responsibility, and often a demand for rights without commitment. Sexual intercourse will need to be seen as the consummation and not the beginning of a relationship.

The church must not adopt society's view of marriage as disposable, and premarital sex as inevitable. Sex is a mysterious union of the physical, emotional and spiritual, which none of us can fully comprehend. Partnership is sealed with

sexual intercourse – the one flesh union, goes far beyond the mere physical…
The one flesh covenant is God's covenant.

Churches may offer support in the following ways:

Teaching

This should include teaching on all aspects of human sexuality, relationships, courtship, marriage, mutuality, responsibility, and the vital need for the power of God's Spirit within our marriage relationships. It is important that issues such as sexual orientation are faced openly and compassionately. There is a clear need for understanding about relationships, that these are far more than merely physical, but involve mind and emotions, and also include a spiritual dimension. There is also a need to deal with the recognition of emotional, spiritual and sexual fulfilment within marriage.

We will need to do some straight teaching from such passages as Gen 2:22-25; Song of Songs; Hosea 1-3; Matt 19:1-15; Jn 4:16-26; 8:1-11; 1 Cor 6:12-7:40 and Eph 5:21-33. Such teaching will be informed through Bible commentaries and books such as those listed in the resource section (p140).

Marriage Preparation

This is all too often a formality, or a cosy chat with the minister. Given the pressures on marriage the church has a heavy responsibility to take preparation very seriously, and insist on attendance at a number of sessions prior to the marriage. This will include discussion about the nature of Christian marriage and the form that the service might take, but should give its main emphasis to the nature of relationships, their development and maintenance.

Time should be given to discussion about understanding each other; accepting people as they are; being reconciled after arguments; bringing different strengths and gifts to a marriage so as to produce a stronger whole; and honest consideration of the wish or otherwise to have children; leisure time pursuits, financial management and responsibility; careers and in-laws. It is particularly crucial to work with couples where one or more of the partners has been married before. The baggage of the previous marriage needs unpacking, understanding and jettisoning where appropriate.

We will need to address the fact that most folk will be sexually experienced, if not actually living together. This means that we will need to move beyond the physical, to a deeper understanding of the biblical basis of relationship. Words like commitment and sacrifice should figure highly. The problems of domestic violence will form a part of this preparation, as we deal realistically with human relationships. We will want to stress the 'something more' that belongs to Christian marriage.

With a Christian couple, discussion should include the place of prayer and Bible study together, and the use of the home for church activities. It is particularly important to stress the need for God's help in our relationships; the fact that we

Almost 4 in 10 first marriages and 1 in 2 second marriages end in divorce.

have been created for relationship, and that God through his Spirit enables us to grow together in understanding and love.

The attendance of church members at a marriage service should be encouraged, as this is part of the church's pastoral care and support for the couple, whether they themselves are church members or not.

For some marriage preparation resources, see the section on p140.

Church Programmes

These will need to take account of the demands of building family relationships. At a time when increasingly both wives and husbands work, evenings and weekends become important in being together as families. The church must therefore be careful in the demands that it makes, consciously or sub-consciously, on attendance at evening meetings and Sunday evening services. Often ministers can make people feel guilty when they stay at home with their partner instead of attending a church event. We should be more imaginative in designing the church programme, so that whole families may be together. We will also recognise the need to encourage the extension of the concept of families so that single people are included. To enable couples, and also lone parents, to attend evening meetings, churches should consider establishing a network of baby-sitters – drawn from the full range of the fellowship and not just single people!

The church might also consider services for the renewal of marriage vows; maybe an annual service for all couples who have been married in that particular church. Couples might also be encouraged to renew their marriage covenant at significant anniversaries, such as 10, 25, 50 years.

Enrichment

More and more people are discovering the value of marriage renewal and enrichment weekends or courses. These are times when couples are given space and assistance to recover an appreciation and delight in each other. There is a Baptist expression of marriage enrichment, along with many other courses. See the resources section on p140.

Counselling

A variety of support agencies for counselling exist, some of which are designed for Christians, some for non-Christians, and some especially for clergy marriages. It is important that we are familiar with a good range of referral contacts so that people can be put in touch with help as soon as a problem arises, rather than having to wait months. A number of useful addresses are listed in the resource section on p140.

The Baptist Area Superintendents have a list of marriage counsellors from other denominations, who will be able to give confidential support and counsel. Every Baptist minister has a list of qualified counsellors who offer a confidential counselling service when ministers' marriages are under pressure.

At a time when marriages are falling apart, what does your church offer by way of marriage preparation?

If you think that it should offer more, how could it be improved?

marriage encounter

Would you recognise the signs of a marriage in trouble?

If you hear of a marriage under stress, what would you do? Would you know where to refer a couple?

THE CHURCH AND SOCIETY

The church's responsibility to ensure that within its own community life God's ideal for marriage is both explained and practised, must be matched by a concern to ensure that within the wider society that ideal is taken seriously. The church may exercise its influence in several ways:

Its Exemplary Witness

Society has every right to expect from Christians in this, as in other areas of life, some correspondence between what is preached and what is practised. A powerful influence, therefore, is for Christians to witness by example to the possibility of strong, lasting and unselfish marriages.

The crucial importance of this witness by example reinforces the emphasis earlier in this chapter on the church's responsibility both to carefully prepare those who seek a church wedding and to actively enrich marriages within the church.

Its Caring Involvement

Many Christians exercise an important ministry within society by their involvement in organisations, agencies or networks, such as those referred to on p140, which support marriages or offer advice, counselling, and care when marriages are under pressure or have broken down.

Churches ought positively to affirm and encourage members whose involvement in the church structures is limited because they represent the church's presence in society's attempts to address important issues and offer care.

Similarly, where caring agencies do not exist locally, the church may explore with others the possibility of setting up a suitable scheme.

▶ Do you know what agencies exist locally, and how well-subscribed they are? Is provision sufficient for your area?

In more informal ways, Christians may extend to neighbours, friends and relatives whose marriages and relationships are under stress a ministry of patient listening, careful understanding and practical support.

Its Prophetic Voice

Statistics at the beginning of both this chapter and the next reveal the extent to which society has moved away from God's ideal for marriage. Christians must find more positive ways of responding to these trends than wringing their hands as it were in condemnation and despair.

The church must not only use its freedom but also accept its responsibility to speak into our culture those values which God intends should shape marriage and which lead to the well-being of men and women within that relationship.

This may mean taking steps to influence legislation which in any way affects marriage and family life by appropriate contact with your local MP and with other leaders in the community. Using existing channels to influence the values, attitudes and assumptions which are expressed in the media is another way through which the church may ensure that the Christian voice is heard.

Notes to leaders

It would be helpful to research the local organisations that support marriages, and have their publicity material available for people. You may also want to talk to your minister to find out what her/his practice is regarding marriage preparation and counselling.

1 Cohabitation is becoming increasingly common. Russell and Sally have been living together for 13 years. They have two children.

"Marriage has never entered my head," said Russell. "I see our future together. We talk about what we will do when the children are grown up. I see us together forever. We are totally committed."

Sally says: "We love each other. Why do we need to declare that to anyone else?"

(Quotations are from a *Mail on Sunday* article: 'Why don't they get married anymore?')

How would your church respond to Russell and Sally's situation if their children started attending Sunday School?
Would you:

☐ Shrug, and say it's up to them
☐ Send the minister round!
☐ Hope they begin to feel guilty
☐ Support them in the commitment they have made

☐ Offer Christ's forgiveness for their sin
☐ Welcome them, with no questions asked
☐ Alert the evangelism team to new contacts
☐ Other …

- Tick the boxes you agree with and discuss your answers with the group.

2 Joan was asked to talk to the youth group about marriage and living together. She said that although sex within marriage was God's ideal, we must recognise that we fail to meet God's ideal in many areas, and we mustn't over-emphasise sexual failings, nor be condemnatory in our attitudes.

Afterwards Brian, the youth leader, was angry with her for not being firm enough in stressing the need for absolute standards.

Two people in the group could act out the ensuing debate between Joan and Brian.
Discuss who was right.

3 A Christian friend confides in you one evening that he and his wife have never had a very satisfying sex life, and he feels increasingly unhappy about it. Somehow, they both feel guilty about uninhibited lovemaking. Maybe it's because they've grown up in a church that somehow gave the impression that sexuality was dirty or unwholesome…he's not sure.

How would you help such a man?
- What do passages such as Genesis 2:24 and Song of Songs 4:1-5 and 5:10-16 have to say about human sexuality?

Belonging

4   Read Ephesisans 5:21-33

     • In this passage marriage is modelled on Christ's relationship with the church. List the words or features this relationship brings to mind, eg, permanance, selflessness.

     • What other important aspects to marriage are described in this passage?

5   Helen and Edward wrote into their marriage service that …*marriage is also for the good of the community* … and they committed themselves to that end.
Whap do you think Helen and Edward meant by this and how might they implement it?

     • Are there some lessons here for you?

6   Is teaching on marriage and sexuality a regular feature of your church's ministry?
Do you think it should be?

     • If so, where would you like to see such teaching taking place? In Sunday worship, special courses?

     • Why?

7   Recognising the high divorce rate, the church has a huge responsibility to ensure both effective marriage preparation and on-going support for couples.

What does your church do, and how could you as a group contribute to this?

     • Do single people have an important contribution in supporting married couples?

8   Would you recognise a marriage under stress? What are some of the signs?

One practical thing I resolve to do
as a result of this study is .....

9   Is marriage a solely private affair or does the church have a right to intervene, if there are indications of problems? What help could be usefully given?

Belonging

Belonging &

DIVORCE

The stigma of divorce prevalent in earlier generations has now gone. What was once hushed-up is now spoken of freely to the point that it is part of the stuff of entertainment, especially in the popular TV programmes. Look at life in the soaps! Greetings cards are now available that specifically relate to those going through divorce. It is a big 'item' in the legal market-place of life, and in the playground too. This chapter looks at some of the issues surrounding divorce and remarriage and at how the church might be more sensitive to these issues.

"Which daddy are you going to this weekend?"
"Oh!" (with regret)
"I've only got one daddy."

Overheard between two six year olds at school.

CHANGING PATTERNS IN SOCIETY

Divorce is a prominent feature of our time and it is on the increase.

- In Britain every year 300,000 people go through divorce.
- 38% of first marriages and 50% of second marriages end this way.
- The chart opposite shows that since 1971 divorces have doubled.
- The duration of marriage is now shorter. In 1984 the Matrimonial and Family Proceedings Act enabled couples to file for divorce after their first wedding anniversary. In 1981 only 1.5% of divorces occurred within 2 years of marriage, but this has risen to almost 10% in 1990.
- Divorces occur most frequently in marriages of 5-9 years.
- For both sexes divorce rates are highest for the 25-29 age group.
- 25% of all divorces involve marriages where at least one partner has been divorced before.
- In 1990 the cost of divorce to Britain was 1.4 billion pounds.
  (These statistics are taken from Social Trends 23 1993).

Marriage vs Divorces

thousands

What are the factors that create new and additional stresses on relationships?

Higher Expectations

People are looking today for more from marriage. No longer is marriage a financial necessity for women, and men and women are more capable of a satisfying independent existence. Consequently people want a great deal from a relationship. This may be fuelled by media imagery which presents relationships in often unrealistic ways.

A Disposable Society

Our society is a 'consumer society'. We purchase and discard commodities as a normal part of life. It may be that relationships today are viewed more as commodities. When they no longer suit or please us, they are binned.

A Sexual Society

The changes in attitudes to sexual behaviour have been very marked over the last 50 years. Far safer methods of contraception and much greater awareness of the possibilities of ever-deeper sexual fulfilment mean that, for the vast majority of the population, sex is no longer confined to marriage.

Questions must be asked if the church is effectively to stem the extent of pain among broken partnerships and their children.

BIBLICAL PERSPECTIVES

We must begin by recognising honestly that interpreting the biblical material is not easy. Christians who differ, sometimes quite fundamentally, on this issue are all sure that they have biblical support for their views. We need, therefore, integrity in holding our views, but also a recognition of the honest and firmly held interpretations of others.

There is widespread consensus about the Bible's witness to God's ideal purpose for marriage, namely the union of one woman with one man for life (Gen 2:24). But concerning matters relating to divorce and remarriage, Christians are not always agreed, either about the meaning of the biblical material or its application to our society and culture.

Old Testament

Certain general principles emerge from considering the Old Testament material and Jewish laws.

● Divorce was permitted, (Deut 24:1-4; Lev 21:7,14; 22:13; Num 30:9), although safeguards existed to avoid a hasty divorce.

● Adultery or even suspected adultery (Num 5:11-31) on the wife's part provided grounds for a husband to divorce his wife (Num 20:10; Deut 22:22).

● A divorced wife was free to remarry, though not to her former husband if subsequently she had married again and had been divorced by her second husband (Deut 24:1-4).

● In later, fifth-century, post-exilic Israel, a woman could also divorce her husband, although God's high ideal for marriage and his displeasure with divorce are still affirmed (Mal 2:15-16).

● Where marriage breakdown did occur, reconciliation was encouraged (Hos 3:1ff; Isa 50:1ff).

Whilst in the Old Testament divorce was permitted, there had to be substantial grounds and a proper legal procedure had to be observed. These factors indicate

Do you think that people are able and prepared to 'invest' in marriage today?

Is divorce too easy an option?

how seriously Jewish society regarded marriage breakdown. If it did occur, then it was no mere private arrangement. Through civil legislation a sense of social responsibility was encouraged. Furthermore, the law protected the rights of the divorced woman.

New Testament

Gospels

In Jesus' day the question about 'grounds for divorce' turned largely on the various interpretations of Deuteronomy 24:1-4. Evidence for differing views among the Pharisees on this issue emerges in their question to Jesus: 'Is it lawful to divorce one's wife for any cause?' (Matt 19:3).

Opinion ranged between the school of Shammai, teaching that a man could only divorce his wife on the grounds of adultery, to the school of Hillel which allowed a man to divorce his wife for any number of petty irritations (such as not cooking to his satisfaction), providing he gave her a certificate of divorce (Matt 5:31). In practice it was probably the view of the school of Hillel which prevailed in Jesus' day, thus making divorce for many trivial reasons quite common.

Cheap plonk again! This time it really is divorce!

Against this background of laxity, Jesus strikingly affirms the teaching that marriage was a gift from God and ideally was for life. Our examination of Jesus' teaching on divorce should be set in the light of his strong reinforcing of that ideal for marriage. For example, Matthew 19 records the reply of Jesus to the Pharisees' question about the grounds for divorce. But note the way he firstly responds by affirming strongly God's good purpose for marriage and its permanence (19:4-6). Given that foundation, Jesus then goes on to concede that because of sin and people's moral powerlessness to live up to God's ideal, the Old Testament permitted divorce. Jesus includes in his reply what has come to be known as the 'exceptive clause' (19:9; cf 5:32), stating that divorce and remarriage are not permissible except where there has been 'marital unfaithfulness' (v9). Jesus does not prescribe divorce in such circumstances, but does permit it.

Perhaps the hardest saying of Jesus is in Mark 10:2-12; cf Luke 16:18, where Jesus calls remarriage after divorce 'adultery'. This is a particular area where Christians with equal integrity disagree. Some see this teaching of Jesus as unambiguous and believe it bans anyone who wants seriously to honour Jesus in this matter from remarrying. Others argue that it is divorce not remarriage which is at the heart of Jesus' condemnation.

...Christians with equal integrity disagree...

Epistles

Paul reaffirms the teaching of Jesus in stressing the permanence of marriage as the ideal (Rom 7:2-3). Death alone releases a husband or wife from the covenant relationship. Once the marriage bond is ended, however, either by death or by divorce on legitimate grounds, then remarriage is permitted (vv2-3).

In 1 Corinthians 7:7-10, having summarised what Jesus taught concerning marriage, Paul echoes the teaching in the Gospels that neither a husband nor a wife should initiate a divorce (vv10-11). Divorce and remarriage, however, are legitimate for a believer whose unbelieving partner may refuse to go on living with him or her (v15).

THE CHURCH AND DIVORCE

In countless marriages love has 'died' or been eroded by betrayal, rejection and a whole category of unresolved hurts gathered over the years, many possibly even before the marriage was embarked upon. What can be offered that is both healing and creative and yet still upholds the ideal of God's intention for marriage?

The main issues for the Christian church centre on the practical issues concerning better support for marriages, sanctioning remarriage in church and the pastoral care of those undergoing or living with divorce.

Support for Marriages

It is important that the church does all it can to prepare people for and support them after marriage, and that the teaching programme of the church covers the areas of life with which people are wrestling. This is covered in more detail in chapter 7.

Remarriage in Church

This is an issue particularly acute in Baptist churches, but has wider ecumenical significance. Anglican and Catholic churches often have policy laid down for them, and couples who have been turned down by these denominations frequently approach the Free Churches as a last resort.

Many Baptist churches refuse to remarry divorcees on the basis of scripture. Others who feel the biblical material is ambiguous also refuse out of respect for the other denominations in the local area. Still others will marry divorcees depending upon the specific circumstances. Usually intensive marriage preparation and counselling would be advised (see chapter 7).

Pastoral Care

Many people who go through the painful experience of marriage breakdown and divorce find a great deal of support from the church family. Sadly others experience a distinct lack of compassion and a sense of alienation.

Understanding Divorce
Part of a church's dilemma when seeking to care for divorced people is the confusion as to what a divorce is.

- Some see it as a positive option; the couple has grown apart and, in order to be honest, they need to modify their marriage vows and end the promise of lifelong commitment.

- Some see it as tragedy or failure, part of our human condition.

- Some see it as sin.

"I felt such a failure … as a woman and as a Christian."

"I was made to feel like an outcast."

Most see it as a confused muddle of these things and are uncertain how to approach those affected by divorce. In order to resolve their difficulties they either refuse to accept what has happened or refuse to deal with either or both parties. This leads to much hurt all round.

In caring for those involved in marriage breakdown a church needs:

- Clarity concerning what it believes about divorce.
- Clarity about all the processes of reconciliation that can be offered – both Christian and secular.
- Awareness of the practical help that could be given to ease the situation. This information can only be gathered on an individual and local basis, but some pointers are offered below under: *Practical Initiatives*.

> How do you view divorce, and what should/can the church offer?

Understanding Divorced People

Caring for those who have become separated or divorced includes recognising the new situation. This will involve awareness of the following factors:

Bereavement. In a marriage break-up the individual usually experiences emotions similar to those of a bereaved person, as well as suffering guilt or rejection, depending on the circumstances. The grieving and recovery period is similar. Divorce is one of life's most painful experiences, yet while society allows the bereaved some two years to come to terms with their loss, the divorced are frequently expected to 'pull themselves together' in a matter of weeks!

New Responsibilities. Whilst domestic duties and financial affairs were shared previously between the couple, each individual now has to cope with learning new skills. Decisions previously shared now have to be made alone. This can be very frightening.

Effect on the Children. This can be a major source of worry, guilt and stress.

Division of Belongings and Friends. Dividing up property and treasured possessions can be fraught, but coping with the torn loyalties of friends and relatives, together with all their emotions, can be even more draining.

Financial Implications. These can be immense, particularly if only one partner worked whilst they were married. Suddenly coping with maintenance payments and benefits can be humiliating, and adjusting to a different lifestyle can cause much resentment.

Longer Term Effects on future partners and families. Increasingly people are living in second or third marriages with children from previous marriages. These are usually a major source of stress in relationships.

A Rite for Divorce

Churches may explore ways of offering to those about to divorce an appropriate form of words which marks the end of the marriage. However, it raises many questions as to how it can be done in ways that are pastorally helpful and theologically sound. The following are some of the issues raised by a rite for divorce.

– If divorce is seen as freedom from an oppressive relationship, there is the fear that the church should not be seen to 'celebrate' a divorce.

– If the emphasis is upon repentance and grace, this takes care of the moral dimension that a covenant has been broken. But why should divorce be singled out as an area of moral failure, over and against other 'sins'?

– If the emphasis is upon death and resurrection, this takes away the heavy moralisation, and the analogy of a funeral avoids appearing to celebrate a divorce. The 'death' of a marriage with all its hopes and dreams is acknowledged and mourned, and a 'resurrection' of a new life and fresh start is prayed for. However, there is some problem in offering the promise of resurrection to a morally ambiguous 'death'.

– If the emphasis is placed on suffering and healing, this allows for fully acknowledging the pain of the event, and for offering healing of the guilt as well as healing of the past.

The advantage of a rite for divorce is that it responds to the following needs of the couple and their children:

- a sense of closure
- forgiveness
- healing
- the community's acknowledgement of the divorce and a pledge to support them as individuals
- a definition of their new status after the divorce

NB Children may or may not wish to participate in the rite and should not be forced. They may wish to write their own statements.

PRACTICAL INITIATIVES

Whilst there are many professional counselling organisations, some people are reluctant to use them, and they often have long waiting lists.

Divorce Recovery Workshop

One alternative that has been pioneered in this country by a Baptist in Maidenhead is Divorce Recovery Workshop.

This is a new approach to the problem suitable for anyone of any age and at any stage of separation or divorce... DRW is a course that deals specifically with helping the individual come to terms with a marriage that has irretrievably broken down. This is accomplished with the use of video material which provides a constructive teaching element, and through small group discussion sessions that offer an environment for understanding personal emotional problems concerning the breakdown of a relationship.

DRW has been so effective that it has developed a national programme which helps groups establish their own ministry locally. For more details contact DRW (address on p141).

Rebuilders Ministry

An alternative model has been developed by Willow Creek – a large community church in Chicago – called Rebuilders Ministry. This is advertised for anyone at any stage of marriage crisis, so that groups include the full spectrum from people who are experiencing stress in their marriage, right through to people who have been divorced a long time. This appears to work in the Willow Creek context, but it requires very able leadership and facilitators. Details from Willow Creek (see page 141).

Family Access and Contact Centres

These are neutral meeting places where children of separated families can enjoy contact with one or both parents, and sometimes other family members. The primary concern of these centres is the child, and the centres aim to make access/contact for the child as free from stress as possible. Many churches have used their buildings effectively for this purpose, and the national network (NACCC) supplies full supporting materials and guidance (see page 141).

Mansfield Road Baptist Church, Nottingham, have been running a centre since September 1993. They are affiliated to the national body and began when an existing centre in Nottingham was oversubscribed with 100 families on their books. They have 24 volunteers on a rota for Saturday afternoons who provide refreshments and care for the children. Referrals come from social workers and solicitors.

Conciliation Service

Conciliation keeps the focus on the children. It involves helping parents, married or not, to find new and manageable ways of parenting their children during and after the break-up of the relationship.

Marilyn Appleton, a conciliation service worker, writes:

> If Jesus were alive in today's world, he would say and do the same as he did 2000 years ago. He would cry over Jerusalem and over many more places... he would surely be out visiting parents who live apart as well as the families where Mum and Dad live together. Jesus would be with those who needed him most.

> Third Way, Nov 1991.

Notes to leaders

You will need large pieces of paper, pens and Bibles. If you are tackling question 8 it may be helpful to have copies of the material in the text under the heading A Rite for Divorce (p63).

1 Think of four divorced people you know and, without naming names, list the main reasons why they split up from their partner.

1

2

3

4

Combine the individual lists on a central piece of paper. Does any one reason stand out as most common?

2 38% of first marriages and 50% of second marriages currently end in divorce. The number of divorces has more than doubled in the last 20 years.

Why has this increase occurred? List some of the factors below and discuss the reasons for their influence.

3 Read Matthew 19:1-12; Mark 10:2-12.

What do these passages tell us about divorce and remarriage?

● What other biblical material would you want to draw on?

4 In pairs, take one or two of the scenarios below and overleaf.

If these people were in your church how would you respond to them, bearing in mind your understanding of scripture. Share your responses with the rest of the group.

Week after week Jane's husband gambles the benefits away, debts mount and eventually the 'phone is cut off. Mounting violence within the home leads Jane to seek refuge in a woman's shelter. Her injuries indicate that the abuse has been long-standing. She is advised to break from the marriage.

What help and advice is available to this woman?

William is a gentle man, in his middle years. His wife seemed to take delight in 'showing him up' at every opportunity. Ridicule and barbed remarks were common when her friends were around. She mocked his commitment to the church, though she was baptised into membership of the local church.

One day he breaks down and weeps, saying he can't take it any longer, and asks you, "Will God forgive me if I divorce her? To live in this house is a slow death." What do you say?

Belonging

Louise (31) has come through a painful divorce. Her husband left her for another woman, and no longer sees their three children (4yrs, 3yrs and 15 months). Louise, although she finds the going very difficult and lonely, says she will never consider another relationship.

George (59) lost his wife last year after nursing her through a long illness. He has met a divorcee from a neighbouring church and has gained a new lease of life. They seem ideally suited, are deeply in love and want to get married in church.

Joanna, a mother of three, is currently having counselling for her own childhood sexual abuse. As her understanding grows, she identifies familiar behavioural patterns in her daughter. It is found that the father is abusing the child. The distraught mother tells you she must divorce her husband. What is your response?

5 It is sometimes hard to strike the right balance between, on the one hand, supporting people who separate and, on the other, not condoning divorce. How do you think your church handles this?

6 List some of the experiences that assail a newly separated person, and then think about whether the church could offer help in easing any of these experiences.

Experience	Help that could be offered

7 What support is offered in the wider community for divorced and separated people?

- How might Christians get involved in these initiatives?
- How could the church help those in the wider community involved in separation and divorce?

One practical thing I resolve to do as a result of this study is .....

8 Some churches offer a rite for divorce – some public acknowledgement of what has happened (though not necessarily involving the whole congregation) – which may include repentance, forgiveness, healing, a sense of a new start, and an opportunity for the wider community to recognise what has happened and pledge support.

Do you think this is a good idea?

- Spend 10 minutes as a group devising a short rite. What elements would you include?

Belonging

Belonging &

PARENTING

What is one of the hardest jobs in the world, which will take a large chunk of your salary, a large part of your energy and time, and will involve you for the next 18 years at least, and at which you have had no previous training?
Answer: *Being a parent.*

It does seem extraordinary that throughout history parents have been expected to absorb this foundational skill in human living and then to undertake the task with minimal support. In this chapter we question this approach and explore ways in which the church can be more sensitive to the current climate and offer to parents encouragement and practical support.

CHANGING PATTERNS IN SOCIETY

Family Unit

Much of the activity and teaching of churches assumes a family unit made up of two parents and their children living together as a stable unit. If the church is to support parents effectively we must recognise that this is not the norm for a large sector of our society.

The statistics below give some indication as to the current situation:

● If the trends continue, by the year 2000 only half of all British children will live with natural parents who were married when they were born and who stay married until they are grown up.

● 1 in 4 children will experience the divorce of their parents before they reach the age of 16.

● 1 in every 3 live births were outside marriage in 1992.

● 1 in 5 of all families with dependent children are lone parents. This reflects an increase of 24% in the four years up to 1991.

● There are 1.3 million lone parents (1.2 million lone mothers).

Attitudes to Children

Not only has the family unit changed, but also have attitudes. Until this century children were 'seen and not heard' until they could be treated as miniature adults. Today there is a much deeper appreciation of the rights and needs of children. We understand much more about child development, and we have a sophisticated culture of childhood which has created its own increasing commercial and media market. This media hype creates new pressures for parents. The financial demands of children can paradoxically lead to their emotional neglect and to dysfunctions in relationships.

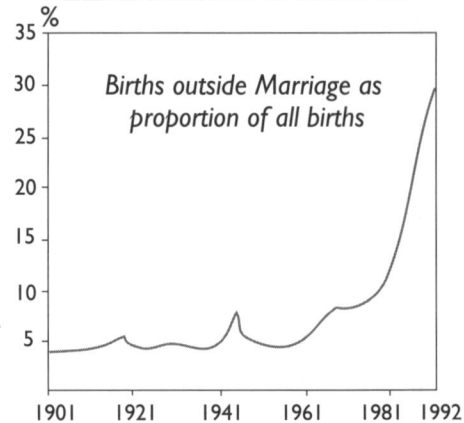

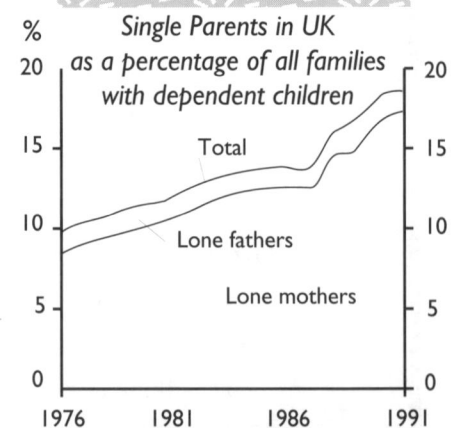

Births outside Marriage as proportion of all births

Single Parents in UK as a percentage of all families with dependent children

Total

Lone fathers

Lone mothers

68

Perceptions of Authority

Similarly, perceptions of authority have shifted. In the past there were much clearer divides between the 'powerful' and the 'powerless', and authority was enforced between these groups in a much harsher manner than would be generally acceptable today. Within families in the past an emotional and physical distancing often promoted obedience and deference to parents. Increasing respect for the individual needs and self-expression of children has rightly softened this approach, but has left a degree of confusion about the place of discipline and the appropriate exercising of authority.

▶ 1. What changes have you noticed in family life and parenting during your lifetime? Is there anything that your parents did that is not so prevalent now?

2. Look at your own congregation – what different styles of family and household are represented?

BIBLICAL PERSPECTIVES

Old Testament

'Family life' was quite different in the Old Testament (see chapter 3). Children were brought up by a much wider network of adults, and the laws and directives that mention children are often primarily concerned with protecting the wider community. We may discover, however, principles relevant to our age.

God as Parent

One of the key contributions of the Bible to a discussion of parenting is its understanding of God as a parent, and most often as a father (Psa 68:5). (For references to the female imagery of God see Deut 32:11; Isa 66:13 and Matt 23:37.) This has crucial significance in shaping our understanding of family, church and society. For some the identification of God with 'father' has been very unhelpful, but for others the imagery of the loving, compassionate provider has been rich and sustaining.

In the Old Testament the status given to the role of father was very significant. One of the prime functions of a man was to have many sons and 'a quiver-full' was a sign of great blessing (Psa 127:3-5). It was out of this context that the understanding of God as the father of the nation emerged (Deut 32:6).

This analogy has often been used to justify all kinds of authoritarian paternalism, but central to understanding the parenthood of God is the Covenant relationship he established with his people – his children. The covenant was the model of right relationship – it arose out of the constant lovingkindness of the Parent (Psa 103:10-14). It was based upon mutual responsibilities, and was dependent upon commitments from both parties.

Specific Directives

These are mainly concerned with teaching children the ways of God (Deut 6:1-9).

Examples of Parenting

Rather than providing us with model examples of family life and parenting, the Old Testament reveals more to us about God's grace in dysfunctional family units. There are numerous incidents of incest, fratricide, favouritism, deceit and betrayal within some of the key biblical families. For example, in the first two chapters of 1 Samuel we read of two parents who prayed for their child, rejoiced at his birth, and dedicated him to God. We read how he came to know God and later became a prophet. However, the very man who taught the boy Samuel about God, and who was instrumental in Samuel's recognition of God's calling, had two sons of his own who were seemingly untouched by Eli's example and who both grew up to be cheats. In many ways these stories give hope to those of us who do not have ideal family relationships – we are assured that we are not beyond the pale. God can still use us, even if things are a struggle at home.

New Testament

In the New Testament Jesus brings the father relationship with God into a new intimacy by his use of the term 'Abba' (Matt 6:9; Mk 14:36). This new relationship is something opened up to believers by the mediation of Jesus alone, and involves a renewing of the covenant, with its same privileges and responsibilities within the 'family' God has created (Rom 8:12-17). However, there is now a closeness of relationship, previously impossible because of our sin. This close, forgiving and loving relationship with God is now the model for human relationships.

Jesus deepens our understanding of the parenthood of God in his parables, with his illustrations of the father's forgiveness and welcome of the prodigal son (Lk 15), and the father's generosity in giving good gifts to his children (Lk 11:11-12).

In the letters we have a number of specific references to parenting that exemplify the mutuality of the covenant relationship between God and humanity.

Children are to be obedient to their parents, but parents are not to provoke their children (Eph 6:1-4).

Parents should provide for their children, give love, security and responsibility with no expectation of return. Parents are also expected to share their faith with their children without exasperating them!

Parents are to manage their households – provide secure frameworks in which children can explore, develop and grow. Also, recognising that New Testament households were considerably larger than today, Christian parents were called to provide an environment which promoted the well-being of the adults also (1 Tim 3:4).

In the NT we read that men who cannot control their own families are not suitable for church leadership (1 Tim 3:5). How does this square with evidence throughout the Bible of God using people despite their failings, whether in family or elsewhere?

THE CHURCH AND PARENTING

Sharing Faith and Values with Our Children

In Baptist churches we dedicate ourselves as parents to God at the Dedication Service, and promise as parents and as a church congregation to nurture and teach our children in such a way that in time they will come to their own faith in Jesus. Many parents struggle, however, with how they can fulfil this responsibility, and there seems little evidence to suggest that churches help them to resolve these difficulties. Consequently, parents often place very high expectations on the church organisations - for example, the Junior Church, and the youth group.

▶ *How does your congregation fulfil the promises made at Dedication Services? What more could it do?*

The following passage, taken from the Church of England's report, *Children in the Way* (1988), may cause us to question our priorities in church life. The report said:

No matter how good the provisions of the local church are for the Christian nurture of the children with whom it has contact, its influence can be negated by the influence of the home... The earliest experiences of life are particularly important. Basic attitudes and assumptions will have been formed by the time the child goes to school.

Even though that person may later consciously reject those attitudes, their influence will remain. The first models which a child has are its parents. Their attitudes as well as their actions will be copied, and foundations of trust and security need to be laid by them.

One of the key lessons which we all need to learn from faith development and other work on the spiritual growth of children is the central influence of parents. This is as true about faith as about every other aspect of a child's development. All those qualities which will enable a child to enter into the processes of faith – the responsibilities of moral thinking, the self-discipline of loving relationships – are rooted in the child's early experience.

We are only just beginning to see how important it is to help parents nurture their child's capacity to respond to the world of mystery, wonder and imagination. We already know that self-esteem and the capacity to enter into caring, loving relationships will flow from early family life, yet we are too diffident or too uncertain to know how best to counsel even Christian families in these matters.

Reproduced by kind permission of National Society/Church House Publishing

Discipline

This seems to be one of the few parenting issues that does get discussed in some of our churches, thanks mainly to the work of James Dobson in books such as *Dare to Discipline*, and *Discipline While you Can*. Dobson advocates a fairly stringent system of disciplining children based on a behaviourist model that rewards good behaviour and punishes bad. He contends that in this way children are conditioned to behave in an acceptable manner. Dobson assumes in his approach that the Christian ideal is that the woman in the household is home all day and that the man (in whom God has vested authority) has the prime responsibility to execute discipline over his children and his wife.

▶ *We recognise that children need clear boundaries if they are to be secure. How should Christians establish these boundaries ?*

Is physical punishment acceptable, and at every age?

Should the father be the main disciplinarian?

Critics would say that behaviourist techniques do not produce mature adults capable of acting in a voluntary rather than a conditioned way. The Sermon on the Mount seems to make it clear that it is not just our outward behaviour but our inner motivation that matters (Matt 5:21-30).

Stresses and Strains

Pressures on parents vary with the ages of the child. The church needs to think through the different pressures parents face as their children grow up (see exercise 4 on the worksheet, p74).

Where can parents discuss such issues in your area?

PRACTICAL INITIATIVES

It may be that we would want our society to be different, but simply condemning the prevailing trends is surely not a sufficient response. At the same time as seeking to provide society with an alternative set of values we also need to minister within the present context.

Parenting Courses

One of the most highly acclaimed courses is that devised by the Family Caring Trust. Their material can be purchased directly from the organisation (see p141) and no particular expertise is needed to run their course. However, you will find that most Anglican dioceses run regular courses, and it may be worth one or two from the church enrolling on an existing course before starting one closer to home. The organisation Exploring Parenthood also provides courses (p141).

Father's Groups

Churches are often fairly good at providing places where mothers can meet and discuss difficulties with their children (although the provision is mainly for women who are not in full-time paid employment). It is increasingly recognised, however, that fathers have a major role in children's development but that they are often ill-equipped to fulfil that role. Despite all the changes in the status of women in recent decades, women are still the primary carers whether or not they have paid work. Many men work long hours away from home and rarely see their children. This has particularly detrimental effects on boys, who may not have any male role models throughout their early years, and possibly up to adolescence. Many men are unhappy about the situation but feel powerless to do anything about it. Churches could host occasional meetings where men discuss their concerns and frustrations as fathers, and pool ideas.

Oh dear! I've missed Bobby's bedtime again...!

Why do we find it culturally acceptable that fathers take a secondary role in child-rearing?

Parent and Toddler Groups

Many churches already run these (in fact nearly 51% of Baptist churches). They can be a very important point of contact between the church and the community, and a place where sensitive ears can pick up the needs of parents under particular stress. It is helpful to have a notice-board that clearly displays contact numbers of local agencies which meet the various family needs – counselling provision, advice on benefits, baby-sitting services, equipment for sale or loan.

Several churches run Toy Libraries alongside toddler groups. The church invests in a number of good quality, robust toys, and then loans them out for a nominal fee on a weekly basis. This can be a great help, particularly to those on low incomes.

Single Parent Groups

Single parents are on the increase and many are extremely isolated and unsupported. Many single parents feel marginalised in church parent and toddler groups, and value the occasional opportunity to get together with other lone parents to discuss their particular concerns. The church can also provide a baby-sitting service for lone parents, enabling them to get out in the evenings and feel less trapped. It is worth noting that lone parents are often financially disadvantaged. Children in single parent families are 20% worse off than those in two-parent households. Around half of divorced or separated mothers and 90% of single, never married mothers are on income support. Poverty can be a major cause of stress, and any sensitive ways of alleviating this could be of lasting value.

Darlington Baptist Church runs a regular group for teenage mums and those expecting babies, to help these very young parents have a place of support where they can find advice and education as needed.

Befrienders Group

As part of the Family Centre run by Stopsley Baptist Church, Luton, in conjunction with Spurgeon's Childcare, the Christian Befrienders Scheme is designed to complement the professional input of the Project with Families in need. Befrienders are drawn from the church congregation and their role is to draw alongside families and individuals offering friendship and practical and emotional support.

Working Mothers

Many women in full-time employment often feel criticised within church circles, either for working at all, or for not seeming to give their full commitment to church activities. Many are effectively doing two full-time jobs, and under a good deal of strain. What support does the church give to mothers who are working away from the home on a full-time basis? How can the church family help?

Support

The church can play an important role in supporting Christians in local agencies, social services, nurseries and schools who work with parents.

Also, the funding of many of the voluntary agencies that offer support to parents is increasingly under threat. How can your church support such groups in your locality?

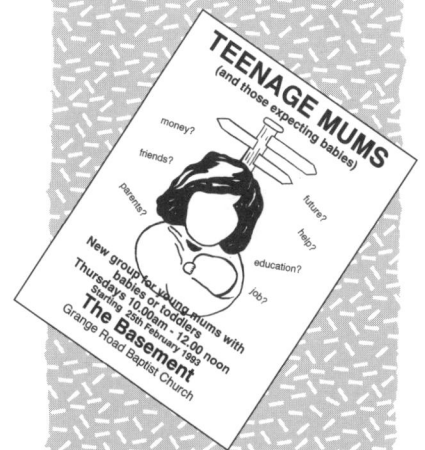

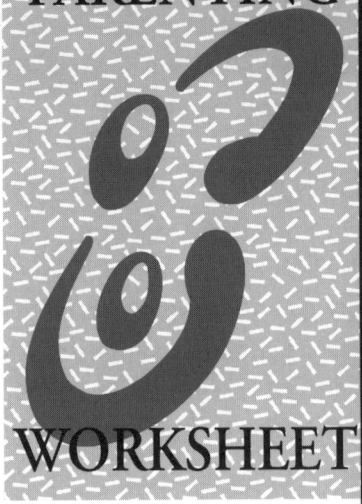

1 Read some of the following passages – Deut 32:6; Psa 68:5; Psa 103: 13; Heb 12:6-11.

How does the imagery of God as father help or hinder your understanding of his character and relationship with you?

● How do you feel about the female/mothering images of God (Isa 42:14; Isa 66:13; Lk 13:34)?

2 The Bible is full of stories about families that don't 'work well'. For example, read Genesis 37:3-11.

What are the effects of favouritism?

● Does this ever happen in families today? How do we avoid it?

3 You have three deacons up for election, all are able Christians, well respected and liked by the congregation:

Irene – a 35 year old single woman

Bob – a 55 year old divorced man whose children have grown up and left home

John – a 40 year old man with a wife and two boys. The boys are going through a rebellious phase, they won't come to church and one is known to be experimenting with drugs.

In the light of 1 Tim 3:8-13 should any of these be eligible for the diaconate?

● What would happen in your church if these people were nominated and why?

4 On the chart below fill in some of the potential strains and pressures on parents at different stages in their child's development, and what support a local church could offer at each stage.

Stage	Pressures and Strains	Support and Resourcing
Early Years		
5-12 yrs		
Teenagers		
Post 18 yrs		

● Where does your church provide support?

5 A couple in the church are preparing for the dedication of their son. They approach Jill (a deacon in the church) and ask her to be a godparent. Jill has several questions:

Is this 'good Baptist' practice?

Is her role to support the child or the parents?

What sort of things would the role involve?

● She turns to you for advice.

Belonging

6 How can we best help our children come to faith?
Tick the boxes you agree with and share your answers with the group.

- ☐ Insist on attendance at church services
- ☐ Be loving parents
- ☐ Annual visit to Spring Harvest (or similar event)
- ☐ Insist they belong to a youth organisation at church
- ☐ Other……

- ☐ Daily 'family prayers' together
- ☐ Send them to a Christian school
- ☐ Live out Christian lives
- ☐ Pray for them

7 Three people could act out the following scenario.

> A 15 year old boy (Gary) arrives home at 12.15 am. He should have been back at 11.00 pm. He has obviously been drinking. It has happened before.
>
> Mum (Jean) and Dad (Paul) are up to greet him. Paul has a tendency to fly off the handle. He thinks Gary needs a jolly good thrashing, but he's too big these days. He wants to ground Gary for the next month, even though this will mean Gary missing the Guns'n'Roses concert he has been saving up for months to see.
>
> Jean thinks this is too harsh and suggests cutting his allowance for a fortnight.
>
> Gary is furious - all his friends stay out until midnight. It's pathetic that his parents haven't anything better to do than dream up punishments for him. He thought Christians were supposed to be loving and forgiving …

- Discuss how the encounter might develop and how it could have been handled differently.
- What similar dilemmas have members of the group faced recently that can be shared?
- What could the wider church family do to ease some of these pressures?

8
> A single parent in her late twenties has three children aged between 2 and 10. She is not involved in her church except that she brings the 2 year old to the church playgroup three times a week. She is living in poverty and by the end of each fortnight finds it impossible to feed her children. 90% of their clothes are bought from jumble sales. She is suffering from depression and finds herself taking out her frustration on her children. Her 10 year old, a boy, is beginning to get into trouble with the police.

One practical thing I resolve to do as a result of this study is …..

- How can you help this woman feed her children without losing her dignity?
- Are there other ways you can help her practically?
- How can you befriend her and show the love of Christ?

9 How could your church help support parents in the wider community?

CHILDREN

Children and adults are made in God's image. Our needs to belong and to live in relationships with others reflect the fact that God is a family or community of three persons: Father, Son and Spirit, who are one. We best experience God's image, the mystery of unity in diversity, by being part of a community. However, the needs of children, including their needs to belong and to share life with others are often forgotten. They can easily find themselves marginalised. This chapter seeks to raise some of the questions that we need to ask ourselves if the church is to be helpful in nurturing amongst children the sense of belonging.

CHANGING PATTERNS IN SOCIETY

Little over 100 years ago children were still being used as chimney sweeps. It was not until 1875 that children gained any significant legal rights. Today we are more conscious of the needs and rights of children, but developments in society and in communications media are prompting us to reconsider how children absorb values and acquire ideas about right and wrong.

The church used to have a very significant role in education through, for example, the Ragged School Union, the founding of Church Schools and the Sunday School movement. Many of our Victorian churches are left with vast 'institute buildings' that used to accommodate huge numbers of children. Today only about 14% of children in England and Wales are in touch with churches. The 1989 English Church Census shows that during the 1980s the drop in children's attendance was even greater than that of adults, even after accounting for demographic changes. It seems that the traditional ways of working with children are no longer helpful. Basically, children have not felt wanted.

The homes in which children are brought up have also changed. Family life has changed dramatically within a generation. While the great majority (98%) live with their natural mothers, many will experience the divorce and remarriage of their parents. Some are born and raised in unstable relationships. 20% of all families with dependent children are now lone parent families. This affects about 2.2 million children.

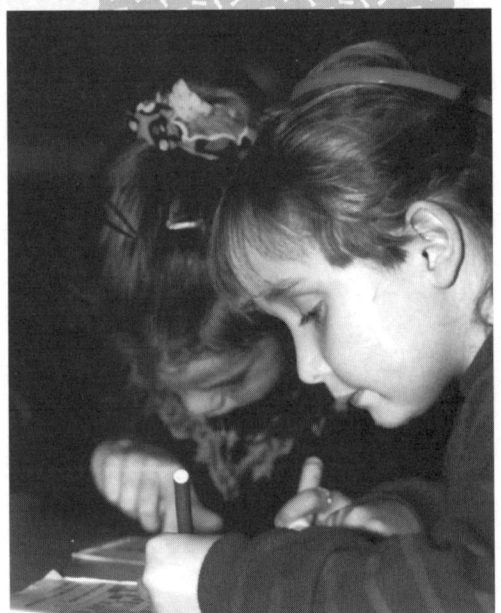

▶ Has the way the church works with children adjusted to these complex changes?

The figures opposite reflect some of the current attitudes to children in our society.

	M	F
It is better not to have children – they are such a heavy burden (disagree)	88	87
Children are more trouble than they are worth (disagree)	86	86
Watching children grow up is one of life's greatest joys (agree)	80	82
Having children interferes too much with the freedom of parents (disagree)	71	73
A marriage without children is not fully complete (agree)	51	41
People who have never had children lead empty lives (agree)	25	22

International Social Attitudes 1994

BIBLICAL PERSPECTIVES

In scripture, as in many cultures, children belong to families which are themselves part of communities, a network of which make up the nation. Children have a clear sense of identity and of belonging. In Israel, children shared with adults in the telling and the living (the remembering) of their faith story (Deut 6:4-7, 20-25). Their significance lay here, that on reaching adulthood they took upon themselves obedience to the law and the preservation of the community's beliefs and values. Jesus grew up and developed in this context. This can be illustrated from the story of his journey to Jerusalem (Lk 2:41-52). The young people were not expected to travel with their parents but were regarded as being safe in the care of the wider community. The fact that God came into this world as a baby and was himself a child, dependent on human parents and family for primary relationships and nurture, affirms childhood in and for itself. When he grew up Jesus founded a new community of people related to one another through their relationship with him – a community that transcended family and tribal borders.

Children clearly liked Jesus' company. They were in the crowds that followed him (Jn 6:9), they praised him in the Temple (Matt 21:16). In part this was because Jesus accepted them (Mk 10:13-16) and described them as models for discipleship (Matt 18:1-5). This was radical behaviour. While Israelites included their children in worship and celebration, they paid them no special attention. They had the potential to become adults, but were not regarded as having intrinsic value or significance; their powerlessness made them marginalised even though they were within the margins of the community. Jesus said of children that 'the kingdom of heaven belongs to such as these'.

Christians variously understand his words. Some believe that children are a part of God's kingdom until they decide against it. Others think that Jesus' words call both adults and children to childlike discipleship. Jesus reveals here something of the nature of God, who gives his kingdom in a totally gratuitous way, against all human calculations. His love for children is therefore 'unreasonable'. Perhaps Jesus used children as an example of the marginal groups for whom God has a particular concern.

THE CHURCH AND CHILDREN

Most children in Baptist churches will have been presented at a Dedication Service. During this ceremony, the congregation promises to pray and care for the child and his or her parents and to be concerned for the well-being of the family. This language makes it clear that the child belongs.

Nevertheless, our behaviour in other contexts suggests that we exclude children.

Children and Worship

Of course, these observations may apply to all the occasions when we gather for worship. Many of our churches have worship designed for children at which adults are present and worship for adults where children are present. Perhaps our mutual belonging and our call to be one community would be better expressed in all-age worship.

Faith in Jesus is personal and needs to find personal expression. However, it is also collective and finds collective expression in the shared worship of the gathered community of believers. Faith is something that grows and finds expression in the context of the community of faith. This must affect the structures we use in which we hope children will begin their faith journey.

Children and Communion

We say that all who love the Lord Jesus may join us in the Lord's Supper. But frequently children are not permitted to participate. This may imply that they are excluded from the family table.

Katie is nine. *It's not fair! No one offered bread and wine to me at the communion service. I'm a Christian – why can't I have it too?*

At Quinton Park Baptist Church, Coventry, the role of the child in the Passover Meal is seen as the model for the participation of children in the contemporary communion service. At Pear Tree Road Baptist Church in Derby, both children and uncommitted adults are present at communion and partake of a 'blessing'.

> What are the ways in which children might be recognised around the table?

Children and Membership

In a similar way, our membership structure and our church meetings exclude children, their questions, ideas and enthusiasm.

> How can we include children in our decision-making process and so nurture their sense of belonging?

Children and Nurture

Evidence points to the fact that traditional patterns of work among children, such as Sunday Schools and uniformed organisations, no longer meet children's needs today. The school/teaching (didactic) model adopted in the Sunday School movement still largely determines our dealings with children in the church today. It is increasingly acknowledged to be inappropriate, yet what are the alternatives? Churches often struggle to attract both children and leaders. Many churches are facing a dilemma.

> How appropriate are traditional Sunday Schools in helping children to come to faith in Christ?

Part of the problem focuses on what a church means by Christian 'nurture'. Is it the unique contribution of the church; that is, the teaching of basic Christian truths, and can this actually be taught in the traditional classroom sense? Or is it the broader aim of ministering to children as whole people and taking on the challenge of contributing to every part of their development – social, physical, emotional and spiritual? If the church chooses the latter course it may have to compete with many better resourced and more popular secular clubs and organisations. If it chooses the former course of action, it radically needs to rethink the pattern and timing of its teaching and its leadership training. Neither are easy options.

What responsibility does the church have for the total development and nurture of children?

A Charter for Children in the Church

1   *Children are equal partners with adults in the life of the church.*

2   *The full diet of Christian worship is for children as well as adults.*

3   *Learning is for the whole church, adults and children.*

4   *Fellowship is for all – each belonging meaningfully to the rest.*

5   *Service is for children to give, as well as adults.*

6   *The call to evangelism comes to all God's people of whatever age.*

7   *The Holy Spirit speaks powerfully through children as well as adults.*

8   *The discovery and development of gifts in children and adults is a key function of the church.*

9   *As a church community we must learn to do only those things in separate age groups which in all conscience we cannot do together.*

10   *The concept of the Priesthood of all Believers includes children.*

Would your church adopt this charter?

If so, how might the congregation need to prepare for it?

What changes in attitude and practice might be necessary?

PRACTICAL INITIATIVES

There is growing evidence that many children today are discouraged, unaffirmed and have low self-esteem. This seems to relate to pressures on family life and lack of relational skills within families. It may result in children feeling unwanted, being alienated from other family members and engaging in unacceptable behaviour.

Are there ways the church can help people to learn or relearn the relational skills required for family living?

Most parents, whether married, cohabiting or lone (divorced or otherwise), want the best for their children. Parents' expectations and children's demands are increasingly high and this causes considerable pressure, guilt and a sense of failure and discouragement. This applies inside and outside of our churches. It seems that families today are attempting to do what only the wider community can do.

As traditional communities, church affiliations and extended families break down, the pressure is placed increasingly on the family unit to provide the sense of belonging, identity and meaningfulness that every human needs. It is small wonder that families are under strain and that many break up. The church must become a pastoral presence in the world, sharing some of the burdens which changes in our culture have placed upon the family unit.

But Dad, if you want a better car wash, we want better pay and conditions.

Opportunities for service among and on behalf of children are legion and Christians have always responded positively to those opportunities. Many

Christians are involved in the educational service, believing that they have the privilege and responsibility of helping to shape the values and development of children. Recent trends in the management of schools have produced increased opportunities for Christians to serve as school governors.

Christians have a long tradition of involvement in service among children who have suffered from neglect, deprivation or disability. Many societies and agencies most honoured by the community have their origins in Christian concern and care (eg, Barnardo's, Children's Society). But through less well-known channels Christians may play their parts in contributing to children's well-being and development. Service as foster parents, involvement with groups offering to care for children whose mothers need to work, leadership of play groups, work with children who have broken the law, service among children in the medical services are some examples of Christians acting as salt and light in the world. More churches are entering partnerships with Spurgeon's Childcare.

The following are further examples of the range of work that is being done.

Vernon Clothing Exchange, Kings Cross, London
A new initiative at the Vernon Family Project is a Clothing Project run in conjunction with Islington Social Services. This aims to provide good quality secondhand children's clothes to families who need them.

Highgate Family Support Centre, Highgate Baptist Church, Birmingham
The Centre offers support to a number of local families through various initiatives, including advice work, adult counselling, playgroup facilities, an out of school project and by acting as a go-between with clients and social services or other authorities. Also available is special counselling for children aged between 4 and 16. The aim is not only to provide support in a crisis but to work to prevent the crisis coming in the first place.

The Buttershaw Christian Family Centre, Bradford
The toy library the Centre runs is pictured in chapter 9, however, this is only one of a range of activities designed to ease the pressures on families on the Buttershaw estate. There are a number of support groups for different ages. There is an 8-12 group for vulnerable youngsters, a weekly parents' group, a craft group and the Anchor club which is an innovative weekly worship group for parents and toddlers. The Centre also provides a visiting scheme for parents.

CHILDREN

WORKSHEET

1 Fill in the chart below, or use a blank sheet if you need more space. Think first about your own childhood – what are the most vivid memories and lasting impressions? Then compare these to what you notice children experience today.

Own childhood memories	Experiences of children today

2

eg Cubs

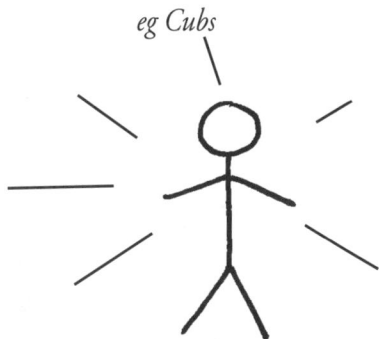

John, 8 years.
Most of his life in care.
Presently with foster parents.

Julie, 11 years.
Lives with her mother
and sees Dad once a month.

Fill in organisations/communities that John and Julie could join that would help their development and nurture their sense of belonging.

● What would each of these networks contribute?

3 Read Mark 10:13-16. This affirms Jesus' acceptance of children. But in what situations would you like to behave like the disciples? Is it OK to feel like this?

4 Katie is nine: *It's not fair! No one offered bread and wine to me at the communion service. I'm a Christian – why can't I have it too?*

How would you respond to Katie?

● What are some of the ways in which children might be recognised around the Table?

Belonging

5 If we say that children are part of today's church and not just tomorrow's, and that they have full rights of belonging, how do we include their ideas and thinking in our church life, when they are excluded from the church meeting?

- Give some examples of situations when the voice of children could be helpfully taken into account.

6 A church in Lower Codswallop is discussing all-age worship. Maureen, the Junior Church leader, is enthusiastic. She says that children are fully part of the church and need to share fully in worship, rather than disappearing to their own classes. Lewis, who has young children himself, says that while he agrees in theory, he feels that the children are a desperate distraction and he can't concentrate on worship. Mrs Jones agrees – she doesn't come to church to pretend to be a butterfly and cut out paper flowers!

What is all-age worship? How do you relate to each of the people above? How would you help this discussion move forward?

7 Amy is 10. Her parents are faithful members of the local church, but they cannot enthuse Amy about church. She is dragged along on Sundays, but finds Sunday School so boring. She has an exhausting programme of activities the rest of the week – gym club, riding, violin lessons, drama group and she is becoming a great computer enthusiast.

Where is she being 'nurtured'? Should her parents be concerned? What more could the church do?

8 Make copies of the Charter for Children on p79 and discuss the questions asked there, in the light of your previous discussion.

9 What facilities exist for children in your local area? Is every age group adequately catered for?

- What do children say they need?

10 What are some of the pressures on families in your locality?

- How might the church address these pressures?

☐ By befriending more families
☐ By getting involved in local play-groups/nurseries
☐ By becoming school governors
☐ By setting up a toy library
☐ By establishing a family centre
☐ By opening a centre for second-hand clothes and equipment
☐ By running an After School Club
☐ By praying for the area
☐ Other......

One practical thing I resolve to do as a result of this study is .....

11 Spend some time praying for those who work with children in your neighbourhood.

Belonging

YOUNG PEOPLE

Young people are front page news but most of the headlines are bad. Does the media hype match up to reality? In order to gain an understanding of the present, it is helpful to recall the past; your past!

This can be done through some of the exercises on the worksheet, p89. The questions are intended to stimulate thinking and application. The suggested activities may be used for a study group or as part of a larger presentation to the whole church.

'Young people' in this chapter refers to those between the ages of 11 and 19, unless otherwise stated.

CHANGING PATTERNS IN SOCIETY

Teenagers are a comparatively recent phenomenon. The term 'teenager' appeared in the early 1950s to define a new economic market ready for exploitation in an increasingly consumer society. Growing economic output required new consumer markets and young people had money.

Young people are under pressure as never before. This pressure comes from a variety of sources:

- **Peers**. Pressure to conform and to belong.
- **Parents**. Pressure to achieve and/or survive family breakdown.
- **Professionals** – ie teachers, youth workers, social workers. Pressure to adopt secular/atheistic philosophies given as fact.
- **Pop music**. Pressure to have something worth following.
- **Programmes and Videos**. Pressure to escape into a world of sex and violence.
- **Publications**. Pressure to follow magazine moral codes promoted as 'advice'.
- **Psychological factors**. Pressure to be loved and accepted in a broken world.
- **Physical desires**. Pressure to be sexually active in the condom culture.

Generalisations in the media blame young people for much of the wrongdoing in today's world. Whilst some young people are guilty, the crimes committed by the adult world against young people are far greater and more damaging. Young people have been robbed of love and true expressions of family, denied innocence and a voice, given poor adult role models and meaningless employment, and exploited by an adult owned consumer world. In short young people have become the powerless generation.

BIBLICAL PERSPECTIVES

Age does not seem to be an issue to God. Throughout the Bible there are examples of God calling the very young, the very old and all ages in between. Examples of those called by God, or used to enable his purposes in the Old Testament include:

Joseph: a 17 year old teenager when God gave him profound and significant dreams (Gen 37: 2).

Gideon: the least important (ie, youngest) member of the family (Jgs 6:15-16).

The young servant girl of Naaman: her faith was instrumental in Naaman's healing (2 Kgs 5).

David: a young boy, prepared to fight when his adult brothers were scared (1 Sam 17:32-33).

King Solomon: considered himself only a child when he began to rule (1 Kgs 3: 7).

Jeremiah: appointed prophet to the nations when only a child (Jer 1:6).

Daniel: a young man who served God in the hottest of situations (Dan 1: 10).

The New Testament is similarly blind to age. For example, God chose Mary, a teenager, to carry his son, Jesus, into the world. The Magnificat reflects her profound spirituality at this early age (Lk 1:46f). Similarly, Jesus was astounding the teachers in the synagogue with his wisdom and understanding when he was only 12 years old (Lk 2:47). Later, after Jesus' death, Peter reminded the people that prophesy would be given to children and visions to young people (Acts 2:17). Paul reinforces this belief when he tells the young Timothy that youth was no barrier to his ministry (1 Tim 4:12). It is clear from other epistles that young people and children were active members of the early church (eg, 1 Jn 2:12-14).

> ▶ How important are young people in the life of your church?

THE CHURCH AND YOUNG PEOPLE

Young people are voting with their feet and leaving the church family at a rate of 900 a week. In 1979, 960,000 young people attended church. Ten years later, only 490,000 remained, representing a net drop of 49%.

If the church were a car, what kind of car would it be?

One teenager's answer was "a Volvo: safe, middle class and boring!"

From the moment that a child is born, she begins to soak up the environment in which she lives. She is taught by parents, friends and members of society the accepted ways of living and behaving.

This process never ends, but as young people grow, they make every attempt to discover their own identity, and try to reject that which is placed upon them by members of their community.

By rejecting other people's expectations, young people are not saying: *We don't want to belong.* They are saying: *We want to belong in our own right, we want to be valued for who we are and the contribution that we can make to this community. We want to feel that we belong, not just to be told we belong.*

> ▶ How have young people shaped your faith?
>
> How can you say to young people "I value your contributions"?

84

Presentation

Tony Campolo says, "the medium is more important than the message". One of the cultural changes we have begun to see in our society is greater informality. This informality is often perceived as irreverent, but if you have ever been to a rock concert or some large gathering of young people, you will quickly notice that they have a great sense of reverence and respect. It is, however, respect that is earned: respect that responds to skill, technical competency and an ability to speak to the audience through some medium of wizardry. You may say: *But they can't understand the words.* But the words are not the most important thing. It is the way the words are communicated that is important. This is what leads young people to say to us: "I haven't a clue what you are talking about. You are so serious. I am just not interested. In fact you are so uninteresting that I don't even want to argue with you."

We need to ask ourselves how are we communicating; what is the message we are communicating to young people? The radical nature of Jesus' teaching ministry, both in methodology and content, attracted people in the same way as young people today are attracted to Guns 'n' Roses, Metallica, Michael Jackson or Madonna.

Motivation

Young people are not renowned for being first up off their seats to help carry the bags of shopping from the car into the house. But they are renowned for being the first to consume the newly purchased groceries. What motivates them to be so keen to do one thing but not the other? In this case the answer is simple. Food. They have empty legs that regularly need to be filled to the top.

The drive is personal need. For many leaders in the church other needs are paramount. We have a need to be wanted by young people and this diverts us from recognising the needs of young people. We are driven to do everything for the young person. For example, we organise the activities, the outings, the food. The young people come along, consume and leave. And we are left to tidy up.

In the minds of young people this is the role of adults. They provide, we consume, they clear up. We have no responsibility for any of the action appertaining to the event.

We need to resist the temptation to satisfy our own needs, and re-focus on the real needs of young people. This involves the costly act of relaxing and ceasing to worry about having loads of activities and programmes, until such time as the desire for these comes from the young people themselves. They then need masses of encouragement and support in achieving their goals.

None of the young people such as Gideon, David and Timothy mentioned above in the Bible passages went to do their task without some form of encouragement. Young people are terrified of failure. It is around them all the time. It is one of the most significant influences upon their lives.

▶ What steps can you take to make the gospel culturally relevant to your young people?

Go up to one young person in your church and ask them to describe to you how they spend their weekend.

Parents are constantly speaking to prevent failure: "Do your homework. Do your revision. Do your studies. Get A+…" Failure petrifies individuals into inactivity. Young people are conscious of failure. They know that the society in which we live has no place for failures.

The church is to be the nest from which young people can fly and fail and return. It is to be the model of Jesus sending out, receiving back, encouraging, educating, reviewing, reflecting in order to send them out again.

Young people, when left to their own devices, will never starve. When given sufficient knowledge on which to base their actions and then left to get on with it, knowing where the resources are, they will not fail. The stories throughout the Bible of young people coming good when they have been given the information, told where the resources are and allowed to get on with it are of exemplary nature.

Go on! You can do it!

Listening

The joke goes: *You have two ears and one mouth, therefore you should listen twice as much as you speak.* During the Year of the Family, the media has been concentrating upon relationships, especially between adolescents and their parents. What is the most difficult thing for parents to do in relation to their children? Many would agree that the answer is *Listen to them.* Studies have proved that most adults ask too many questions and hear too few replies.

Questions of interest become an inquisition, during which the young person invariably shouts and leaves the room to no one's satisfaction.

This might be one occasion when the joke is nearer the truth than we might think. It is often assumed that young people don't like talking. The music is too loud, so how can they ever have a conversation? They only mumble and grumble. Yet if you actually talk to any group of young people they will tell you that they have the most animated and interesting conversations. Young people today are probably less tolerant of irrelevant drivel than ever. The reason is that they have been educated on such a high level of quality input: television, radio – and if you throw up your hands in disgust, it just shows how prejudiced you are!

Young people enjoy conversation, talking and listening, especially to genuinely interested adults, who they normally find rarely want to listen to what they have to say. They are so full of what is in their own head, that they cannot hear what anyone else is saying.

In what ways do you allow young people room to work out their faith within the life of your church?

How can you help young people to be creators, not consumers?

How good a listener am I?

What steps can I take in my church to improve my ability to listen to other people?

PRACTICAL INITIATIVES

Relational Youth Work

Whilst the church has lost significant numbers of young people, so too have other structured youth organisations. The traditional youth club is no longer effective. Young people are more impressed by meaningful relationships than organised programmes. Nothing is more powerful than an adult who takes a genuine interest in young people. This is real family life.

Detached youth work is a youth club without walls. Missionary youth workers venture into young people's territory, bringing Good News on the streets. This is vulnerable and demanding work but the rewards are great.

We made contact with them within the youth centre and in various pubs in the neighbourhood. Their level of acceptance of us ranged considerably from individual to individual, some were friendly, some wise-cracking and skitty, some avoided us completely, some were openly hostile. It was easier to get to know the fringe members of the group rather than the six young men at the gang's core – their exterior hardness was difficult to penetrate.
Just as we had got to know the young people, it was important also to develop relationships with other professionals in the area – to get to know them as people, rather than as social workers, school teachers or probation officers.

from *Street Mates*, Jude Wild

Disciple Orientated Youth Work

Discipleship is about lifestyle, not just Bible knowledge. A church which ventures onto the streets must be prepared to accept into the family young people who have no experience of church or Christian behaviour. Habits formed since birth rarely change instantly. This requires patience and understanding from established family members, as well as consistent discipline and encouragement.

I've just discovered something completely amazing: an activity which has turned Michael – usually a loud and disruptive 17 year old – into an efficient organising machine. What is it? A meal. A meal … for 120 people from our church. The key elements in this rather surprising discovery seem to be: (1) it was his idea; (2) he wanted to get everyone involved; (3) it's going to be fun, but have a purpose (serving the church and giving the profits to charity).

Simon Hall, Youth Worker, Moortown Baptist Church, Leeds

Gareth, known on the streets as 'Brad', would never consider going to church or youth club but some 'Street Pastors' got involved in his troubled life. They accepted and loved him. Gareth and a number of his crowd eventually became active family members of Chawn Hill Christian Centre.

Gareth was different to those who already attended church. His clothes, hairstyle, criminal record, behaviour and Christian experience singled him out as being different. The 'Waffle Group' (a discipleship and nurture group) provided opportunity to meet, in a secure family environment, with other young people where he could come to terms with his new faith. The Waffle Group allowed for doubt, failure, discussion, prayer and application of the Christian life.

Cultural Youth Work

Youth workers are missionaries reaching lost tribes of young people from different cultural backgrounds. Missionary youth workers must contextualize the gospel. This will vary according to target age group, region and current trend.

Culturally relevant programmes need to follow relational youth work, not vice versa.

Emmanuel Baptist Church, Gravesend.

Emmanuel runs a monthly youth worship service called No Limits. The service takes a magazine approach and uses media and technology to which young people relate. On arrival drinks are available from the non-alcoholic bar, followed by worship and biblical teaching on youth-friendly themes involving live music, drama, street dance, interviews, large video screens, computer graphics and theatrical lighting.

The No Limits events take a great deal of planning and preparation. Emmanuel is helping young people to get involved in this at every stage from conception to presentation. Ideas, material, rehearsal, organisation, decor, T-shirts, technical operations, video editing, lighting rigs, stewarding, bar-tending and 101 other things are covered by a large team of young people.

Geoff Cook, Youth Ministry Worker

YOUNG PEOPLE

WORKSHEET

1 Show what you have brought to the rest of the group and briefly share what memories the item evokes.

2 When you were young, what were the times when you had both a strong sense of belonging, and a great sense of isolation?

- How do these reflections help, or hinder, you to understand the feelings of young people today?

3 Think of young people who have influenced your life positively – taught you, challenged you, enriched you.

- Think of young people who have made the world a better place.

4 It is said that young people are under pressure as never before – do you think this is true?
- What are the pressures – list them on a central piece of paper.

5 Darren is a member of the youth group at church. Darren's friends all say they are sleeping with girls, and like them he carries condoms on him 'just in case'. His mum, Jenny, finds the condoms one day while hoovering his room.

Ask two people to act out the scene when Jenny confronts Darren, and then discuss how young people can deal with some of the pressures they feel.

Some of Dave's friends at church come to the youth leader to tell her that Dave is selling 'soft' drugs at school. He has been bullied by some of the older boys. He denies using the drugs, but his friends say that he certainly behaves stoned at times. His parents know nothing, but are getting at him about his falling school work standards.

How could the church best help Dave?

Belonging

6 How does the Bible view young people – are there examples of God using the young?

- What do you learn from this about the way your church handles the ministry of young people?

7 Many young people are striving for a sense of belonging – to be accepted as they are, with all their differences.

- What actions could you take in the church context that say to young people: 'I value you and your contribution'?

8 If the church were a car, what kind would it be? Compare your answers to those of the teenager from Stourbridge (p84).

9 The use of choruses in church services began in the 1960s as a response to major changes in contemporary music expressed by the Beatles and Simon & Garfunkel. Much current worship music is still based on past folk music and not contemporary styles. Do you know what music is in the charts at present? (You could play the video clip here if you have one.)

- How concerned are we to make worship relevant to young people?

10 At many church meetings we hear moans about the decline in the numbers of young people.

- Why do we want young people in the church? Whose needs are we meeting?

11 Being listened to is valued by people of all ages, particularly the young. How much are young people listened to in your church?

- How much do you listen to young people?

One practical thing I resolve to do as a result of this study is .....

12 How much are we prepared to risk in enabling young people to work out their faith in church?

- What sort of things might change?
- What changes could you make to your own actions and attitudes?

Belonging

Belonging &

OLDER PEOPLE

'Will you still need me when I'm sixty-four?' That line from the Beatles' song echoes the concerns of this chapter which looks at the way churches, shaped by biblical principles and responsive to contemporary social patterns and trends, may offer to older people a sense of belonging, value and dignity.

CHANGING PATTERNS IN SOCIETY

We Are an Ageing Nation

Largely as a result of improved public health measures and diet, a greater proportion of the population than ever before belongs to the group designated 'elderly' (men over 65 and women over 60). This trend will continue.

In 1991 there were 10.6 million pensioners. By 2031 the numbers are expected to increase by 38% to over 15 million.

Perhaps more significantly, the number of 'old old' (those over 75) has risen and now comprises 36% of all the elderly. In 1901 there were 57,000 people over 85 living in the United Kingdom. By 2001 there will be 1.2 million – a phenomenal increase in a very vulnerable group in society.

Several consequences for the elderly arise from the present national, social and economic situation. Large numbers of active elderly people, some with comfortable pensions, create demand, for example, for holidays abroad and further education, whilst others are hard up and their lives are consequently restricted.

An important demographic trend in the 1990's is an increase in the proportion of elderly people living alone. 61% of women aged 75 or over live alone and the Department of the Environment projects a net increase of over 600,000 elderly single person households between 1986 and 2001. This has major implications for health and care services, because living alone is the largest demographic risk factor – after age itself – of admission to hospital or entry into a long term care home.

Many widows live alone and are desperately lonely. Thousands of house-bound and handicapped people struggle on without adequate support. Increasing numbers of frail elderly people and those who are mentally confused swamp the welfare services. More and more 'young elderly' who are caring for parents in their eighties and nineties are under enormous strain.

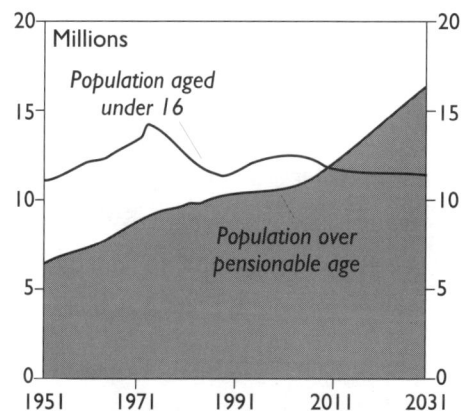

Millions. Population aged under 16. Population over pensionable age. 1951 1971 1991 2011 2031

How do you react to the facts about our ageing population? Does it make you fearful in any way? Why?

Most housing cannot accommodate multi-generational living. Many elderly no longer live near their families because of increased population movement. Family breakdown and subsequent remarriage create complex extended family patterns. It is often difficult to know where the grandparents belong in the new order. Younger women do not always choose to be the 'carers' of elderly relatives (indeed those younger women may well be the bread winners in their family unit).

Any room for me, dear?

More people are being made redundant in their forties and fifties and are unlikely to be re-employed. Increasing numbers of early-retired people, especially men, are bored. Because fewer people are in work, the financial resources are not being created to provide the increasing numbers of pensions and the care needed by the dependent elderly.

For women, the breakdown of marriage, bringing up children on social security, loss of years in employment and probability of only part-time work being available, results in greatly reduced pension rights and very low income in retirement years.

BIBLICAL PERSPECTIVES

The Bible affirms that individuals, at whatever stage of life, are of infinite value and worth to God. That foundational principle is illustrated clearly in Psalms 71 and 139. Much biblical material about older people reflects cultures in which old age was considered a blessing from the Lord (Gen 15:15; 25:8; Judges 8:32; 1 Chron 29:28; Joshua 14:10-11) and the elderly were respected and honoured (Ex 20:12; Lev 19:32; Prov 23:22; 1 Tim 5:1-2).

But the Bible acknowledges honestly the feelings of weakness, humiliation and even rejection experienced by the elderly (Psa 71:9). On the other hand, there is an equally strong emphasis on God's promise to remain constant in love and care 'even to your old age and grey hairs...' (Isa 46:4).

Biblical material concerning the elderly frequently emphasises their positive contribution in ministry and service, both within and beyond the community of faith (1 Sam 2:22; Psa 71:18; Psa 92:14; Psa 148:12-13).

Anna and Simeon are singled out as two elderly people who played significant roles in the events surrounding the birth and early life of Jesus (Lk 2:25-38). The Book of Acts picks up the promise of Joel 2:28 that in 'the Day of the Lord' the elderly will be among those who see God's purposes and discern his will (Acts 2:17).

THE CHURCH AND OLDER PEOPLE

Ministry to Older People

● Part of a church's responsibility is to help people understand and prepare for the experience of growing old. Elderly people often face an identity crisis as changing patterns of relationships and roles press on them questions about who they are and where they belong. The church has a crucial responsibility in enabling the elderly to respond positively to new experiences, helping people, for example, whose lives have been filled with work to adapt to new patterns of living. In summary, the church must work out the implications for people in old age of the Christian message of 'wholeness'.

- Other aspects of ministry to the elderly have a practical emphasis. Churches can ensure that their buildings are easily accessible to the less mobile. Providing ramps, appropriate toilet accommodation, stair lifts, well-placed spaces for wheelchairs, and sets of purpose designed cutlery and crockery when food and drink are served, are examples of practical ways in which churches may help the elderly towards a better sense of belonging.

- Churches need to plan activities, whenever possible, to include the frail elderly, providing transport and designating someone to welcome them and to attend to their needs.

- The elderly are helped when churches give meticulous attention to details concerning information sharing. For example, a church may ensure that each elderly person has a 'link' member who personally takes to the older person the church newsletter, weekly notice-sheet or invitations to special events. The 'link' member may tell him or her what has happened at the church meeting and stay to have a time of prayer about the news and information shared. To pray together whilst holding hands is a powerful experience of fellowship – the importance of human touch cannot be over-estimated. If the church has a tape ministry, then one or two members sitting and listening to the tape with an elderly person is very effective, especially as the elderly are often ill at ease in operating audio equipment. It is important to give training to those who visit the elderly. Recent research reveals that communicating news and information to the elderly requires three presentations, each in a slightly different way.

No, no no – the chip in the FM oscillator has gone…

- Churches also need to evaluate if infirm and house-bound people receive adequate pastoral care (the house-bound might mean the carer). Leaders should share with the church when there are insufficient people exercising this ministry.

- Churches may consider organising home communion for the house-bound at the same time as communion is celebrated in the gathered church. Home communion sets may be prepared and laid on the communion table in the church. At an arranged point in the service some deacons (and others) may come forward to receive those sets and the church can pray for those to whom communion will be taken. The deacons will then go to the house-bound where communion can be celebrated simultaneously. This practice has proved to be well worth the practical planning and effort.

- It is important to review organisations particularly designed for the elderly. Are these organisations doing the best possible job and if not, in what ways could they be improved? Could they do more to widen horizons or to exercise a more specific Christian witness?

> We are all on a spiritual journey and this pilgrimage idea implies change and progress. In what ways might elderly people be expected to still develop and grow in their faith and experience?
> How may churches help older people to continue growing and developing?

Ministry by the Elderly

Belonging is not one-way. The elderly are not just on the receiving end but have much to offer. It is important for elderly Christians to express their Christian faith and commitment, even if their capacity for active participation has been greatly reduced. It is important, therefore, for churches to enable the elderly to contribute and thus to increase their sense of belonging.

The elderly bring two major gifts to the Christian community.

Experience

The over eighties have inevitably lived with bereavement and loss of family members and friends; fast moving technological advances; changes in attitudes and expectations concerning every sphere of life; and the changing role of men and women in the church and the community. We must explore ways of using this experience.

Reminiscence Groups — reflecting on and evaluating life experiences and faith. Sharing the results of that reflection in worship, or in the church magazine.

Befriending — twinning an elderly person with a young Christian. An older person is more likely to be at home when the younger person needs to pop in and talk about a question or doubt. We underestimate the witness of the elderly.

Sharing Skills — with the young through badge-work in youth organisations.

Hospitality — people living alone often find food preparation unrewarding because they eat on their own. Could a useful two-way ministry be encouraged by suggesting they share a meal by inviting another person on a regular basis, and that hospitality is shared in return, especially if a Christian invites a non-Christian.

Could a house-group be held in an elderly person's home? Take care that the practical preparation isn't a burden. Perhaps a more physically able person who can't offer their own home could help with the preparation and be a 'hospitality partner'.

There is much talk currently about every member being gifted for some aspect of ministry and service. What factors might tend to make a church exclude older members from the exercise of discerning and realising gifts?

TO THINK ABOUT

Erik Erikson observed despair among the elderly and then wrote in detail about that despair and the causes of a sense of increasing futility that some adults experience with ageing. He emphasised that there might be connections between the low status of old persons in contemporary Western culture and the lack of direction or sense of meaning that afflicts our adolescents. Erikson put forward a concept that generations are profoundly dependent on one another; unless the young have before them a personification of fulfilment in old age – actual evidence of respected and self-respecting old people – the young members of the community cannot develop a sense of purposeful sequence in the different phases during a lifetime. Lacking this, their own development as individuals can fail to take form and direction. The young person seeks an identity for herself, which she can be helped to find if in her society the aged have a defined place and a valued role. There is then a visible representation of each stage of life, including the last. If in this sequence the elderly are overlooked or actively disregarded, their neglect endangers 'the sense of life and the meaning of death' necessary for society as a whole.

Available Time

Many older people long to use more time in Christian service. This may mean involvement as a prayer partner. This implies the careful selection of specific people and issues for them to pray about. It is vital that they are kept regularly and intelligently informed. But the elderly also may be involved in pastoral care. They may be linked to specific people with whom they keep in touch by phone or by letter. (In the latter case particularly with young folk away at college and link missionaries.) It is important to be sensitive to such matters as reimbursing costs where necessary.

In general, nurturing a sense of belonging in the elderly through pastoral care and by creating possibilities for their involvement needs more organising and discipline than we are normally prepared to acknowledge. But by not doing so the church loses a rich diversity of people and resources.

The Elderly in the Community

The European Year of Older People and Solidarity Between Generations (1993) established four objectives – combating ageism, volunteering, promoting health and removing barriers to social and environmental integration. These and other initiatives may be the focus for the involvement of many Christians and congregations in the wider community.

Combating Ageism

We have already discussed attitudes within the church, but should there be legislation that protects the rights of older people; that makes age discrimination an offence?

Volunteering

Numerous opportunities exist to work alongside older people in the community – befriending, meals on wheels, respite care, simple maintenance jobs and financial advice. A church could gather the different possibilities and display them on a special board, so that people could see what is needed. The Citizens Advice Bureau and local social services will provide useful information.

Promoting Health

If loneliness and isolation are major factors in diminishing the physical well-being of older people, then there are many 'neighbourly' things that we can do to ensure older people around us look after themselves properly, gain access to any services they need and are informed of any benefits to which they may be entitled. Why not invite someone from social services or Age Concern to present an evening on practical ways of caring?

Removing Barriers to Social and Environmental Integration

A Christian group could gather information concerning what older people think about the community's provision for their needs. Issues like public transport, shopping facilities, leisure and recreation provision, the design of houses and household goods, are all areas which are of vital importance to older people. Planners and designers often do not take account of the views and needs of older people. Yet older people can form powerful pressure and lobbying groups, providing facts and energies can be well organised and channelled.

> What steps could a church take to recognise, equip and train redundant and early-retired Christians for service in the church and community?

> How can your church make the fullest use of the older members of the congregation in its work and witness?

95

PRACTICAL INITIATIVES

Holiday at Home (Didcot Baptist Church)

This is a week in the church calendar when a group of people arrange activities for older people in the community who, for one reason or another, no longer get away from home for a holiday.

Didcot Baptist Church run it from Tuesday to Friday during the week following the Spring Bank Holiday. There is a break on Saturday and they finish on Sunday with a cream tea and evening service in the church when favourite hymns are chosen by the guests.

Activities include lunch with the mayor, local history talks, an outing with picnic, music and singing, a coffee morning and a variety of input from church members and local celebrities.

It has worked very well for the last few years and is an excellent means of contact with the community.

Centre for Afro-Caribbean Elders (Wolverhampton)

Members of the small congregations of Progressive Baptists in Wolverhampton recognised that the needs of Afro-Caribbean senior citizens were not being met by the community. They established a day centre, open five days a week, that caters for over 50 people a day. The majority of members get to the centre by means of transportation provided by the project. Whilst at the centre the senior citizens are provided with a hot meal, and have the opportunity to participate in a variety of craft and recreational activities – supervised by a trained occupational therapist funded by social services. The centre makes a huge difference to those attending.

In addition the project also provides an outreach Home Support Service to older people and to other house-bound disabled members of the community. This service exists to provide practical support – light household chores, meal preparation, simple maintenance tasks – and advice, particularly on welfare benefits, and advocacy when necessary.

Initiative in Dementia Care

One in 20 people over 65 and one in five over 80 are affected by dementia – the 'quiet epidemic'. A Christian Working Group on Dementia has recently been established to inform the churches about dementia and promote practical Christian responses to the needs of sufferers and their carers. The group includes people in nursing, social work, geriatric medicine, and old age psychiatry. It aims to collect information about existing Christian initiatives and stimulate theological reflection on dementia. Further details from the group's convenor: Bob Baldwin, York House, Manchester Royal Infirmary, Oxford Road, Manchester M13 9BX.

Notes to leaders

You will need Bibles and several large sheets of paper. It will be helpful to collect information about local organisations, activities and facilities for older people.

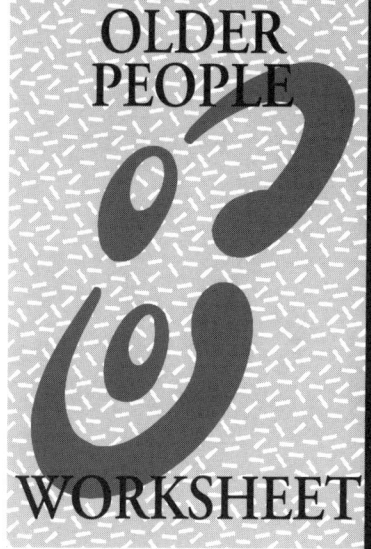

1 List some of your hopes for your own 'Old Age'.

Share them with the group. Now list some of the realities in the experiences of older people known to you.

● Are there differences between these two lists? Why?

2 The number of older people is growing as a proportion of society. In 1991 there were 10.6 million pensioners. By 2031 there will be 14.6 million (1 in 5 of the population).
● What do these facts make you feel?
● What are the financial implications for society and for the church of increasing numbers of older people?

3 What factors have you noticed in society today that make the lives of older people more lonely and that diminish the sense of belonging?

4 What do the following scriptures teach us about the Bible's attitude to old age?

Gen 15:15	Exod 20:12	Lev 19:32
Josh 14:10-11	1 Sam 2:22	Ps 71:9
Ps 92:14	Prov 23:22	Isa 46:4
1 Tim 5:1, 9-10		

5 Read Luke 2:25-38.

● How do the experiences of Anna and Simeon illustrate some of the biblical promises and assurances about growing old?

● How may we apply these promises and assurances to older people today?

● Is age a barrier to Christian service?

Belonging

6 How do older people spend their time in your local area? Pool your ideas on a central piece of paper.

● What are some of the felt needs of older people in your community?

● How would you go about discovering more accurately the answers to these questions?

7 Older people are a growing but often marginalised group of people. In what ways could your church begin to help meet some of their needs and strengthen their sense of belonging within the community?

8 *Our society is infinitely richer because so many people enjoy an active old age. This is something to celebrate.* Taken from a leaflet published by Age Concern.

List ways by which older people have enriched:

● Your life

● Your church's life

● The life of your local community

9 Is the tendency inevitable in our society to view older people as 'receivers' rather than givers? Make two columns on a large sheet of paper and list:

What your church gives to older people	What your church receives from older people

● What steps could your church take to:
(i) ensure the lists are more in balance
(ii) encourage older people to see that they still have valuable contributions to make?

One practical thing I resolve to do as a result of this study is .....

10 Imagine you wake up on the first day of your retirement from full-time paid employment.

What are some of the things you might be thinking about which could significantly diminish your sense of belonging?

● Does your church do anything to assist this 'rite of passage'?

● What sort of things might be helpful?

Belonging

MULTI-CULTURAL COMMUNITY

Britain's multi-cultural society offers a challenging context for the church to live out its conviction that the gospel is for all people and that in God's sight each person is of infinite value.

This chapter explores the implications of this conviction, exposing the prejudices which deny the gospel and offering practical suggestions for encouraging multi-cultural community.

CHANGING PATTERNS IN SOCIETY

The Historical Perspective

So far as may be discerned from the historical records, the population of Britain has always been culturally and ethnically diverse. Traditionally, the British have regarded themselves as being of Celtic, Roman, Anglo-Saxon and/or French-Norman descent. But even this range ignores the minority groups who have lived in these islands for centuries; many of our cities have long-established Jewish communities; there have been black communities in some of our major cities for many years. Irish immigrants built, among other things, the network of canals around the country; the examples could be multiplied. Britain has always been to a greater or to a lesser extent, multi-cultural.

Since the end of the Second World War, the pattern of British urban life, if not that of the whole nation, has been altered again, this time by two successive periods of immigration by non-Europeans. The first of these began in the 1950s when the British government invited people from the Caribbean to assist with post-war economic recovery. The second started in the 1960s and was of people from the Indian sub-continent. These periods of immigration, and the reaction to them, created considerable social upheaval. There was widespread and well-documented hostility towards the immigrants.

The Current Scene

In many respects race relations in Britain have improved over the years but racially motivated discrimination and violence remain major social problems.

99

The charts below reflect the continuing economic disadvantage of many ethnic groups in Britain.

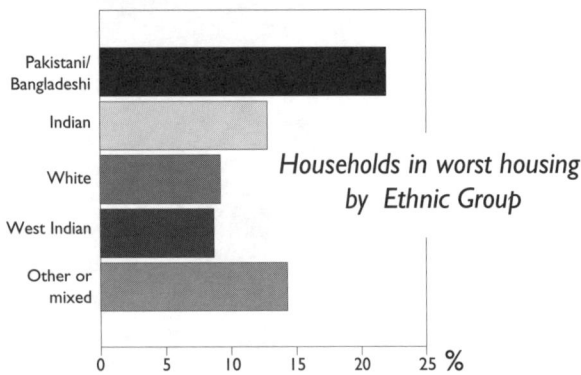

Households in worst housing by Ethnic Group

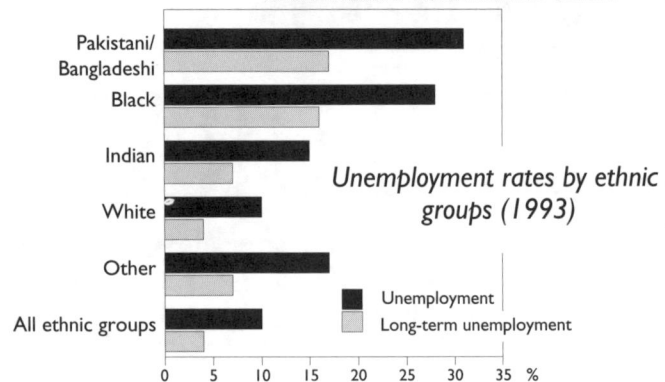

Unemployment rates by ethnic groups (1993)

We are confronted by conflicting evidence. On the one hand, Parliament has introduced legislation designed to protect individuals from racial discrimination; there is clear evidence of greater tolerance towards different cultures; more members of ethnic minorities exercise positions of responsibility in public life (for example, the number of black MPs is increasing, albeit slowly). On the other hand, society as a whole continues to manifest and to tolerate racist attitudes: for example, the difficulties experienced by the black conservative candidate in Cheltenham at the last general election; the election in the Isle of Dogs of a councillor representing the British National Party; the continuing racial abuse of black footballers by some sections of supporters; the increasing amount of anti-semitism manifested in attacks on synagogues and Jewish cemeteries.

Clearly, there are grounds for concern as well as signs of hope and of encouragement.

▶ What is the state of race relations in Britain today? Is there equality between the races? Do we ourselves harbour prejudice?

BIBLICAL PERSPECTIVES

Old Testament

It is easy to read the Old Testament as though God singles out one specific race for preferential treatment, and that the response of that race to their special standing before God was to shun or to destroy the other races with whom they came into contact. In fact, this is a very superficial understanding of Old Testament faith; the creation demonstrates God's desire to have a relationship with all humanity; the choice of Israel was not deliberately exclusive but had a purpose that involved the other nations, namely that God's chosen people should be 'a light to the Gentiles'. This calling was ultimately fulfilled in the coming of the Messiah (Isa 42:6; 49:6). Two of the Old Testament's shorter books reveal interesting and contrasting attitudes towards foreigners. The book of Jonah reveals the failure of the Jewish people to carry out this aspect of their calling; the prophet Jonah articulates their exclusive attitudes (Jn 4:1-3). On the other hand, the book of Ruth illustrates how a community welcomed a foreigner and how she became integrated into a family, a society and into the great plans of God.

The Gospels

Christ came for the salvation of the whole world (Jn 3:16-17). It is true that his mission focuses on the Jewish people (Matt 10:6; 15:24), but Jesus demonstrated great compassion for and sensitivity towards those outside the Jewish community; the Samaritan woman (Jn 4:1-42), the Syro-Phoenician woman (Mk 7: 24-30) and the Roman centurion (Lk 7:1-10). Furthermore, Jesus commissioned his disciples to go to all nations (Matt 28:19-20) and promised them his presence and the power of the Spirit of God as they went to the ends of the earth (Acts 1:8).

The Early Church

The early church had to struggle to grasp and to retain a vision of itself as a community of both Jews and Gentiles. The conversion of Gentiles caused some difficulty (see the story of Peter and Cornelius in Acts 10) as did attempts to integrate them into communities of Jewish Christians, some of whom believed that Gentiles needed to adopt Jewish cultural identity, that is assimilate, if they were to be part of the church. This issue is addressed by the Jerusalem Council in Acts 15 and by Paul in his letter to the Galatians. Paul, as apostle to the Gentiles, argued consistently for the idea of the church as one multi-racial community (Eph 2:14-16; Gal 3:28).

▶ In the light of the practice and teaching of the early church, can there be any biblical justification for the presence of all-black and all-white churches in the same community?

THE CHURCH AND MULTICULTURAL LIFE

Mono or Multi-cultural Churches?

The arrival in Britain of many West Indians in the late 1950s and early 1960s presented our churches with a great opportunity for integrating black Christians, many of whom were converted through British missionary endeavour, into the life of our fellowships. Sadly this opportunity was largely missed. West Indians were told in words and by manner, in churches throughout urban Britain, that they were not wanted. British Baptists were happy to support missionary work in the Caribbean, but apparently did not wish to see people from the Caribbean settle in their churches. In many cases the rejection was not conscious or articulated but was nevertheless communicated to the newly arrived West Indians.

Regarding mono-cultural churches:
I believe we have lost the focus of the gospel – God's reconciling power.

It reminds me of the white Christian sailor in Roots who went on a slave cargo ship to earn enough money to get married. The church growth philosophy of homogeneity is a heresy that, like that young sailor, has sacrificed principle for expediency. That approach has encouraged the separation of the church rather than reconcilation with God, each other, and the world – which is the church's mission.

John Perkins

In many cases, the more unreceptive churches became declining white communities in the midst of the cultural upheaval around. Of course there were exceptions and a few churches made serious attempts to welcome West Indians and to integrate them into the life of the church. Black deacons and

▶ Is the growth of mono-ethnic churches to be regretted? Can anything now be done?

101

occasionally assistant pastors were appointed. These foundations enabled churches to welcome the many new racial groups who have since settled in their area.

However, in addition to some genuinely multi-racial churches, large numbers of mono-ethnic churches have developed and there are many exclusively Caribbean, African and white congregations ministering to their own sections of the population.

Discrimination – Myth or Reality?

During the 1980s both liberal and evangelical wings of the church were concerned to reaffirm the New Testament vision of the church as a community that transcends racial and cultural distinctions. However, there remain causes for concern: our churches appear to be strongest where the local ethnic minority presence is low. For example, the Baptist Union Directory shows that of the 14 London Baptist Association churches that have more than 250 members, 10 are in affluent, mainly middle-class suburbs. A recent survey of the leadership of the denomination revealed that over 98% of Baptist leadership was white.

Spring Harvest, attended by many Baptists, is a strongly middle-class, Anglo-Saxon event. This may be due to the price which excludes poorer Christians generally, and such factors can reinforce discrimination.

The number of black pastors is minimal and many white ministers are reticent about living and pastoring in communities that are ethnically mixed.

▶ Should ministers, perhaps as part of their training, be required to serve in multi-cultural areas?

Responding to the Challenge

Christians who wish to respond to these issues need to cross a number of barriers.

The Pain Barrier

No one has cornered the market on prejudice. Many of us experience difficulty in communicating with, ministering to and being ministered to by people of different cultures. All of us have the potential to make racially-motivated generalisations and assumptions; we are, in Christ, a new creation but we are also creatures of our own age, context and culture.

Christian conversion should lead to an ability to criticise our own culture and to challenge the negative assumptions we make about others. Jesus challenged such assumptions when he told the story of the Good Samaritan (Lk 10:25-37), and Paul taught that our minds should be renewed so that we no longer conform to this world's patterns (Rom 12:2).

Baptist Times

The People Barrier

If we believe that God's purpose is to build a church that unites all peoples and yet we choose to worship and associate only within our own ethnic group, then our actions contradict the hope of the gospel. Friendships across cultural divisions are a means of breaking down prejudice, but may involve some effort.

▶ Do we, like Peter in his dealings with Cornelius, need to confront our own prejudice and confront the pain caused by exclusion and racism before we can contribute to the building of God's multi-cultural church?

The Cultural Barrier

We are inclined to think of rural Anglican churches as inherently English or revealing the real Britain. There are certainly positive things to be said for expressions of national and cultural identity, but many of our churches do not reflect the surrounding community and are behind rather than ahead of any changes going on within them. Often church life is geared for the white population and is imposed upon other racial and cultural groups. If we are serious about building cross-cultural churches, we need experimental creativity in the cultural experiences of church life; this may involve, for example, musical styles, use of non-English prayers and songs, non-English speaking preachers, talking through interpreters and celebrations of diversity in food and dress and so on.

▶ **Are we willing to try to build genuine and lasting friendships with people of different races and cultures from ourselves?**

The Church Barrier

Many non-Christians see mono-ethnic churches as legitimate religious expressions of different parts of our society but also see them as evidence of the inability of Christians to unite the races. Integration cannot come overnight, but some degree of co-operation in the direction of integration may be a sensible first step. For example, the mono-ethnic churches in a given neighbourhood may come under a common umbrella organisation or resources may be shared between churches.

▶ **Are there ways we can experiment so as to change the cultural expression of the life of our churches?**

We should never forget that God is building a kingdom for all people and that our destiny is to share in heavenly worship with people from the whole world, gathered together around the throne of the Lamb (Rev 7:9).

▶ **Is it fair to regard cross-cultural or multi-cultural worship as a foretaste of the heavenly worship described in the Book of Revelation?**

Reflections from Newham

It is tempting to have an idealistic picture of the local church in a multi-cultural area providing a true community. But the reality is somewhat different. Networks of national communities can cut across church allegiances. It would seem that many people in such congregations are finding real community and a sense of belonging from their own national support groups or friendship networks. They come together only on a Sunday morning for an experience of Christian worship and community.

In this particular church, some of the Ghanaians worship also with a Ghanaian congregation as well, where the worship is in their tribal language. Some Tamil Christians also attend a Tamil speaking congregation. A Punjabi Indian group also go to a Punjabi speaking fellowship. So even in what appears to be a truly multi-cultural congregation, certain needs can only be satisfied beyond the church community.

Graham Routley
Baptist Minister

PRACTICAL INITIATIVES

Tackling the Roots of Racism and Racial Prejudice

There are a number of organisations that help churches and other bodies become more aware of their attitudes and discriminatory structures. The Baptist Union staff at Didcot have been on courses provided by MELRAW. There are also locally based groups of Baptists in the West Midlands and south London who are looking at racism in our churches. (For contacts and addresses see page 143.)

The cost of training courses can be reduced by sharing the day with other churches in the area. (Though groups of more than 20 are not recommended.)

Hospitality

The growing number of refugee and ethnic churches means a continual pressure on meeting space. Baptist congregations could look at the possibility of offering their premises for these new fellowships and to developing relationships with them.

From Newham:

> *This particular church is not unusual in that it has four congregations other than its own which use the premises every week. This is an important way of helping independent congregations to belong, although there will sometimes be great difficulty dealing with an African church which wants to use the premises in ways which are different to the normal.*

As well as church fellowships there are often black and Asian community groups looking for a meeting space during the week.

Broadening Cultural Experiences

Whether a church is in a multi-cultural area or not, it can be helpful to 'internationalise' experiences in worship, music and food. Whilst people equate the 'familiar' with 'superior' a barrier exists. The more such prejudices can be broken down, the more open people may be to receive new ideas and new people. Resources exist in the development agencies – Oxfam, Christian Aid, Tearfund – which indicate recipes, music and worship resources from other countries and cultures which can enrich the experience of congregations and deepen appreciation.

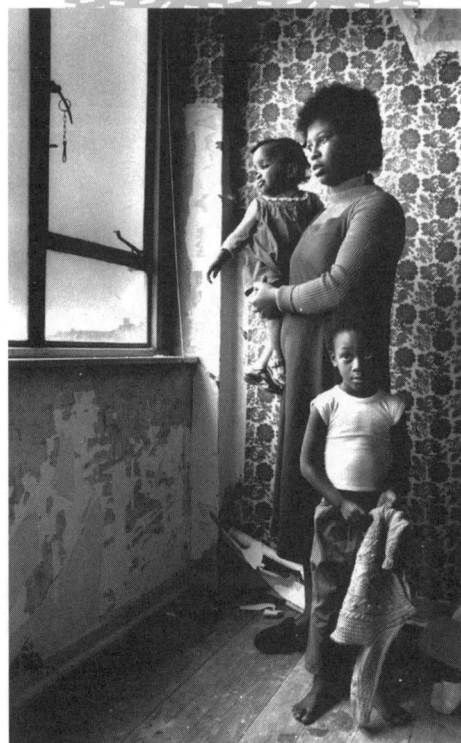

John Twinning

Recognising Economic Difficulties

Factors such as higher rates of unemployment amongst ethnic groupings mean that schemes that give practical assistance to families that are hard up are often the most useful. Again, from Newham:

We are aware in our part of London of the fragmentation of society, and of people who are marginalised. Folk who are not only unemployed, but not employable, for example. There is a real ministry for a church in making its premises available to people; so that the model of the church serving the people becomes a building open all week and staffed as a drop-in centre; a Good as New Shop which becomes regularly used by folk on low incomes; a Parent and Toddler Group. Around all of these initiatives cluster small communities of people.

The point about this is that the local church congregation by their presence and giving enable the premises to be used in this way, and may provide a few people to run or relate to these activities. You have to take a risk and see what will happen.

There are also challenges to the way we time church meetings – for example: do they consistently exclude those doing shift work? Are there ways in which we can alternate timings so that one group does not get excluded?

Another means of tackling the economic disadvantage felt by ethnic communities is for churches to 'prefer' black firms for building, cleaning and repair contracts.

Telling our stories

A church in Battersea deliberately set aside time to hear people's stories and share their experience of church. This gave opportunity to people who never normally spoke in church meetings, and it was remembered as one of the most moving events in the church's life, and significant in building understanding between the different ethnic groups.

Diagram for use in exercise 2 of the worksheet.

Place a red dot for where you were born
2 blue dots for where your parents were born
4 green dots for where your grandparents were born

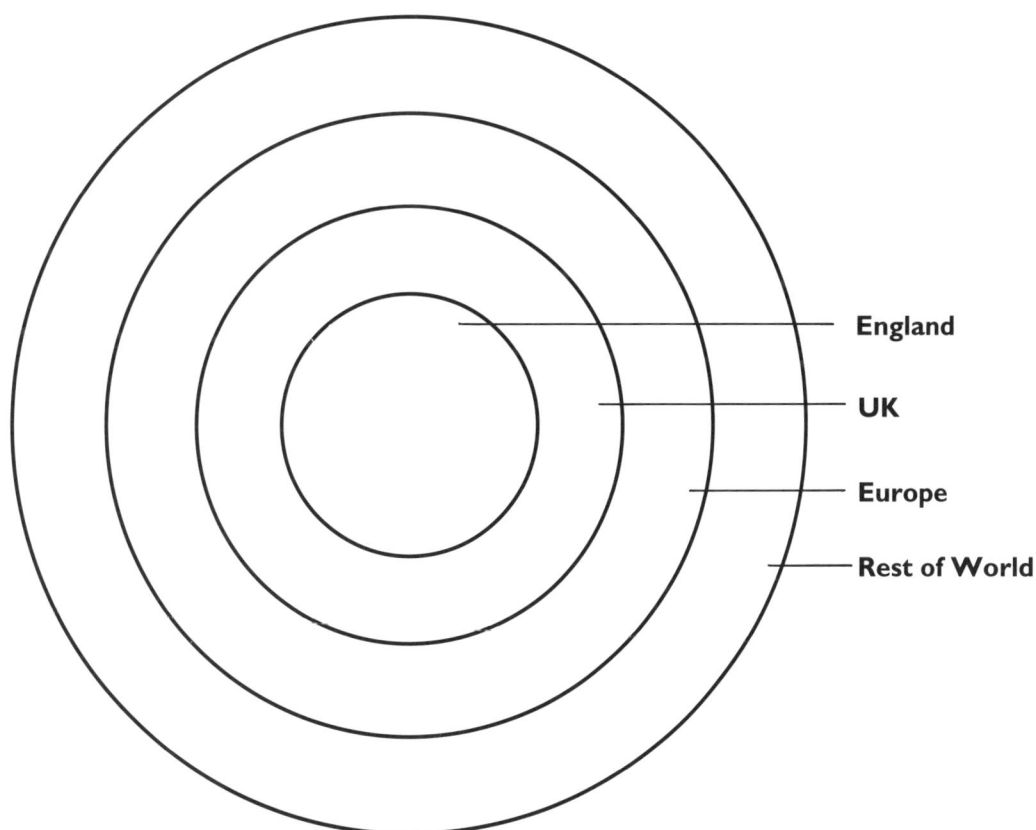

England

UK

Europe

Rest of World

Note to leaders

Before the meeting reproduce the diagram on p105 on a large sheet of paper for use with question 2.

You will also need Bibles and felt pens of 3 colours or stickers (dots) of 3 different colours, eg, 1 red, 2 blue and 4 green for each person.

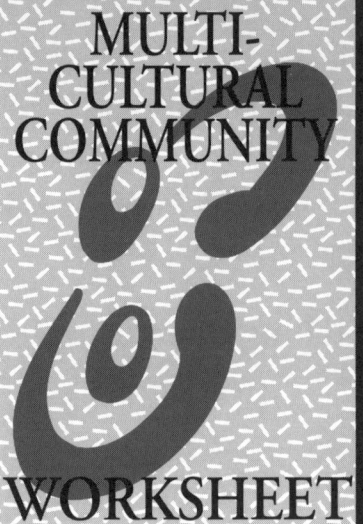

1 Britain today is 'multi-cultural'.

How would you define this?

- What indications of this are you aware of in your own experience?
- How has this affected your life?

2 Think about where the following were born: yourself, your parents and your grandparents. Using different colours for each generation mark your origins on the diagram provided by your leader.

3 Despite having been ethnically diverse for many years, racism is still evident in Britain. What examples can you list?

- Can you identify any racist attitudes in yourself?

4 When you picture the scene in the Garden of Eden, what colour are Adam and Eve?
- What colour do you think Jesus was?
- Is it important that Jesus was Jewish? Do you agree that he was Jewish?
- What do you learn from your answers?

5 Look up Galatians 3:28 and Revelation 7:9-10.

Do these verses add to our understanding of the church – how?

Belonging

6 Jesus focused primarily on the nation of Israel but there are many examples of him ministering to individuals of different races and faiths.

How do you think the church would model Jesus' response to the following contemporary parallels?

Text	Contemporary example	Jesus' Response
Roman Centurion (Lk 7:1-10)	A Muslim leader who asks the church for help	
The Syro-Phoenician woman (Mk7: 24-30)	A Tamil refugee who needs money to bring her daughter over to this country	
The Samaritan woman (Jn 4:1-42)	One of the wives of an African pastor who wants to teach in Sunday School	

7 There has been phenomenal growth in the number of ethnic churches in the UK. Some argue that homogenous churches (ie, all of one cultural group) are inevitable and to be encouraged for effective church growth. Others see this as heresy (see quote on p101).

● What can you identify as the advantages and disadvantages of mono-cultural churches?

8
> When working in a Lancashire town with a largely Pakistani community a pastor was approached by a Shia Muslim family asking if they might use his church hall as a resting place for a deceased relative so that friends could come and pay their last respects. They had no access, or felt they hadn't, to the Sunni mosques and so approached a Christian for help. The pastor believed that it was not only the natural human thing, but also the biblical precept of offering hospitality, that obliged him to respond positively.

What might have been some of the consequences of that action for the pastor, the church and the Shia Muslim family? What would your church have done?

9 At present, black pastors and leaders only account for a tiny fraction of the leadership in our Baptist churches (1.59%). Is this racism in our denominational structures, or is there some other explanation?

● Whatever causes you have identified, how can we encourage more multi-cultural leadership and greater participation by all racial groups in denominational life?

One practical thing I resolve to do as a result of this study is .....

10 Regardless of where you are located geographically, what could you do in the next 6 months as a church, or as individuals, that would give expression to the multi-cultural reality of the church, or increase appreciation of different cultures?

Belonging

Belonging &

DISABILITY

Our Christian faith tells us that we are all 'disabled' by sin, failure and the harsh circumstances of life. None of us are whole; we all have scars and vulnerabilities. Some are visible, others are hidden, but the great hope of Christianity is that in Christ we are all on the road to wholeness, and one day we will be 'perfected' in God's grace.

For the purposes of this chapter, however, we are specifically looking at the particular needs and contributions of people with permanent mental and/or physical conditions that result in specific difficulties.

CHANGING PATTERNS IN SOCIETY

In many ways society is better informed about and more appreciative of people with disabilities than at any other time in history. The movement away from using disparaging terms, the improved facilities in many public buildings and the statutory provision are testimony to a more caring and supportive approach.

A few specially designed toilets and ramps, however, are not the end of the story. Improving physical access is obviously necessary but access more generally to every sphere of life and living is still a major issue. Our level of understanding and involvement is very superficial. Churches are by no means in the forefront of improvements in access and attitudes. Many Victorian churches with imposing steps up to the entrance do not see disabled access as a sufficient priority to merit the expense of changing the approach.

Many churches also see people with disabilities at the receiving end of care rather than as individuals who have much to offer to the life of the community. There is obviously much for us to learn.

- There are 6.5 million disabled people in Britain.

- 1 in 5 households include an ill or disabled dependent.

- 1 in 19 people were registered in 1992 as 'substantially or permanently handicapped'.

- 1 in 100 babies in Britain has a mental disability, eg, cerebral palsy affects 1500 babies a year, Down's syndrome affects 1 in 700 babies born.

Who do you regard as 'disabled' in your church?

What is the basis of your answer? How do you define disability?

In biblical times and until quite recently, children born with severe physical and mental disabilities would have died quite early. Those with very limited intellectual ability but physically fit would have fitted into the labour intensive, manual work of communities more easily than in today's hi-tech world.

People often treated those with psychiatric illnesses as demon possessed and treated them accordingly. Thus we must view the biblical material carefully. Rather than looking for examples of specific instances involving disabled people there are some more general principles worth focusing on.

God Looks on the Heart – 1 Samuel 16:7

This passage makes it clear that whilst we so often judge people by external features, these are totally irrelevant to God. He is interested in our inner lives. Similarly, the great 'Servant' passage in Isaiah 53 speaks of the Lord's servant being so physically marred that people found it hard to look at him, and yet he is the supreme instrument of salvation.

God Works through Weakness –
2 Corinthians 12:7-10

Paul does not make clear what his 'thorn in the flesh' actually was, but his repeated prayers for its removal met with a negative response, so he had to live with his own imperfections and troubles. He concluded through his pain and limitations that he, and all believers, had a great deal to learn from not being perfect. God's message to him was *My grace is all you need for my power is strongest when you are weak.*

Jesus greatly respected the apparently weakest and poorest members of his society, because their vulnerability and dependence revealed much about the Kingdom of God. His teaching was all about love and inclusiveness.

Society values the strong and the perfect, but Christian faith stands against this. How can we practically live out this understanding in our Christian lives?

Healing and Wholeness

Whilst it is clear that Jesus had an amazing healing ministry, and healed some people with profound disabilities (eg, the man covered with leprosy (Lk 5:12f) and Legion (Lk 8:26f) who would be considered mentally ill today), there is a danger that we assume that healing is the only truly 'Christian' option. Whilst the New Testament writers focus naturally on the miraculous, it is clear that many people who came into contact with Jesus were not physically or mentally healed. The miracles were signs that pointed to who Jesus was and to the values of his Kingdom. They were not meant to dominate our perception of Jesus' priorities (cf Lk 4:23-27).

THE CHURCH AND DISABILITY

The church needs in its own attitudes and practice to model both what it believes about people's value in God's sight and the love which seeks all people's well-being and growth towards wholeness. The following are some important factors which the church needs to take on board.

Respecting the Individual

Too often people can cast all those with disabilities into one category and not give time learning to understand and appreciate each person's individuality. Sentimental, patronising attitudes (the 'Does he take sugar?' syndrome) can be very painful – they may require help, but ask them first what would be most useful. Too often we rush in and 'help' without fully appreciating the effort and hard work someone may have put into mastering a skill. However slow and painful it may be to watch, we need to respect that person's pride and independence, and admire their determined efforts. A good example is resisting the temptation to finish the sentence of someone who stammers. This increases the frustration and nervousness, and so makes the stammer more pronounced.

Recognising the Needs of the Whole Family

▶

A family with a member experiencing any severe disability will find that the whole family is affected, especially if the disabled person is at home. The mother of a severely disabled woman writes of

> ...help so desperately needed and never received from the church. We had a strong faith which stood us in good stead. But what people don't understand is that the whole family is handicapped. And it's very important that people understand that, especially the church. But ministers shy away from the subject: they don't know what to say.

Another man deeply involved in the life of his church observed that in the 34 years of his autistic son's life

> ...only on one occcasion have prayers been said for him in our church.

The church should be aware of:

Isolation

A family with a child who has profound and multiple disabilities will be very tied. Going out is a major operation, and often an ordeal. Parents can feel embarrassed by their child's behaviour and wish to expose the child and themselves to as little public attention as possible. They may feel it hard to relate to other parents and the more isolated they become, the harder it is to sustain any external relationships. Leaving a child with a 'sitter' can be very difficult for parents; they do not wish to impose their burdens upon others. Those seeking to support these families need to be aware of these feelings, and convincing in their willingness to share in the care. It may take a while for a sitter to learn the special needs of the individual concerned. Those with a disabled member of the family may find more acceptance and help in a Disability Support group, where people

How able is your minister and pastoral team to deal sensitively with disability issues?

In what ways does your church support families with disabled members?

really understand the pressures, than in the church. This can result in a conflict of loyalties for a Christian family. Those who do remain committed to a church can find themselves very isolated from the rest of society.

Exhaustion

Caring for a person with severe disabilities can be very draining. Nights are frequently broken, and often the disabled individual drains a carer's physical and emotional resources. Carers may feel they have nothing left to give anyone else.

Conflicting Emotions

Brothers and sisters of a disabled child, however hard their parents try to avoid this, can easily feel neglected, and suffer from the restrictions placed on family life. They may struggle with many conflicting emotions of love and resentment. They need time in their own right, both from their parents and from the church community, and opportunities to occasionally escape.

Financial Pressures

The special equipment and resources that make life easier or fuller can be very expensive and swallow up much of a family's or individual's income. Also, disabled adults mostly live on limited state benefits. This needs to be borne in mind in relation to social activities that require tickets or fares.

Examining the Church's Accessibility

Are the physical characteristics of your church user-friendly for all? Churches need honestly and courageously to examine their buildings and activities from the point of view of disabled people.

Physical characteristics

* **Wheelchair access** – ramps, wide doors, toilet provision, space in the sanctuary.

* **Access** for those who have difficulty walking – ramps, grab rails, space reserved near the door.

* **Hard of hearing** – loop system, signing provision, particular sensitivity at social activities. People with hearing aids often have to turn them off in situations where there is a good deal of conversation and extraneous sounds, as they cannot filter the noise and it can become unbearable. This is often not understood, and creates unnecessary irritation.

* **Sight difficulties** – large print books, talking books, tape ministry, clearly marked stairs. Some churches have braille hymnbooks.

I think Molly's picking up Radio Singalong on the loop system, again.

* **Accessibility of toilets** – many conditions make staying in church for a full hour impossible. Often toilets are only accessible by going out in front of the entire congregation which is too embarrassing for many.

* **Provision** for those who cannot read.

There are many organisations that can help with the design and building of churches. See the resources section (p143).

How would you rate your church's accessibility and sensitivity to disabled people on a scale of 1-10?

Activities

In planning its activities, events and programmes, churches should strive to ensure:

● **Acceptance** of disabled people and their maximum integration with minimum fuss.

When you think about church activities, how many help those with various disabilities to belong? For example, what would you say to two mentally handicapped adults who attend Sunday worship regularly and want to receive communion?

> *In the week leading up to his baptism Stephen (who has Down's syndrome) sat for a total of six hours and painstakingly wrote to every instructor at the Training centre inviting them to the service. .....His face was radiant as he came out of the water and said for all to hear "I did it – I've been baptised". And what a witness it was, as every one of his instructors, most of them non-Christians, had responded to his invitation...*
>
> from *Let Love be Genuine* ed. F.Bowers BU 1985

● **Accessible Christian Nurture Material**

BUiLD booklets, for example, are written especially for those with learning difficulties or literacy problems. The organisation Causeway produces Bible study material, with training materials about how to set up a group, (the *DIY Training pack – the Local Church and People with Mental Handicaps*) and markets a special 'Easy to Read' version of the Bible.

● **Sensitive Practices**

Churches should establish and maintain sensitivity in their practices and language. For example, consider the effect if the first words a wheelchair user hears on entering a church are:

Let us stand and worship God.

A better practice might be illustrated by the words heard in a Guildford church: *If you want to commit yourself to this, either stand or move your wheelchair forward a foot or so.*

Causeway produce a Christian Awareness pack, which includes a tape. There is also a complementary video, and a specially commissioned album of music and songs produced by Adrian Snell. This helps churches begin to understand the issues better.

The church must also regard disabled people as participants and not merely spectators in the congregation's life. For example, the Causeway group at Harlow Baptist Church have found that they have acting talents, and interpret biblical stories, mimed to music. Friends from their day centre, and local shops came to church to see them tell the Christmas and Easter stories. Their version of the Good Samaritan, where eventually a dirty old man, drunk and homeless, renders assistance to the shopper overtaken by an epileptic fit, is both hilarious and hard-hitting.

Members of Harlow Baptist Church

PRACTICAL INITIATIVES

The Community Care Act that came into being in April 1993 furthered the process of placing people with mental disabilities and illnesses into homes and hostels in the community rather than in big institutions which often locked them away from the wider society. Many people have been dislocated by this as, often, the placement is inadequately resourced. Some spend their time wandering between GPs, social workers, prisons and churches – lonely and threatened. The community in its turn is inadequately prepared to understand the needs of these people and often feels threatened by them. Churches need to join with others in becoming aware of the crisis and discovering the best ways to care for one another in the neighbourhood.

Get Informed and Ask for Training ▶

People to turn to may be:

- Local social services department

- Your Community Health Council

- Chaplains in local hospitals for those with mental illnesses or disabilities, or the Community Chaplains

- The local or national office of MIND (the association for mental health)

- MENCAP (the national association for people with learning difficulties)

- Carers National Association which campaigns for and works with carers

- Local Christian Social Responsibility Officers (SROs), eg, some of our own Baptist Association representatives or the Anglican diocesan SROs

On opening its Open House Centre, Manvers Street Baptist Church in Bath felt that members needed training in understanding people with mental illnesses and the best way to care for them. They invited staff from the Mental Health Unit at the local hospital to put on a day's workshop. 22 people attended, and it was considered a very worthwhile day –

"I learnt some facts about mental illness that I was totally unaware of."

"I'm not so scared now."

"I realised what a thin line there was between balance and imbalance."

"It was good to hear that we should not bite off more than we could chew, and that there was professional help that we could and should ask for."

A further day is planned dealing with violence and aggression.

Involvement

Involve at an early stage in the discussions those for whom the care is intended. Too often churches start initiatives without appropriate consultation, to the detriment and embarrassment of everybody.

Political Action

Practical responses are important, but Christians must also speak out about the adequacy of the national community care policy and its funding. It is essential that provision is monitored locally, and churches can have a vital role in pressing for a better service.

Church-based or Individual Activities

A Befriending Scheme – This is probably one of the most important things that a church can do, and it can make all the difference to individuals who are struggling to cope in the community.

A Drop-In Club

The Kingfisher Club at Tonbridge Baptist Church meets fortnightly. Initial contacts were made through local schools for children with special needs. Members of the church, and from other churches in the town, volunteered to help.

The club began with the enthusiasm of one church member who saw a need to provide opportunity for a club where children with learning difficulties could meet together socially and enjoy themselves. It was recognised that this would also give some parents the occasional break from the care of their children and this has certainly been appreciated.

So do you need special qualifications to help the Kingfisher Club? I believe the answer to be No, but the ability to get alongside a child or young person with learning difficulties, a sense of humour, patience, stamina – these will all be needed. What a joy it was to see a Tonbridge Baptist Church member in her eighties enjoying a game of Connect with a teenage girl with learning difficulties. Who was giving? Who was receiving? It would be difficult to say, but we thank God for this opportunity of serving the community in this way in Jesus' name.

Susan Wright

A Carers Group – perhaps starting with people you know already.

Respite Cover – This is organised by many local authority social services for individual families, and they are always short of volunteers who will offer a day, a week or a month, when the disabled child can be looked after to give the parents a break, or time with their other children.

An alternative approach is that of Dagnall Street Baptist Church, St Albans who, once a quarter, organise a Fun Day for people with mental handicaps. Nearly half the membership of the church are in some way involved in the day.

A Self-help Group

Advocacy Support – This may be part of the befriending work, but it can also be a specialist ministry helping people to fill in forms, deal with authorities, and sort out benefit claims.

Links with a Group Home or Hostel – It may be that the church can develop a relationship with an existing hostel nearby.

Bushey Baptist Church in Watford has an occasional lunch at the church when the residents and staff of a local home come and relax. This began through the initiative of one of the housegroups – *'We approached this with a degree of apprehension. Face to face with these people, how would we cope? What could we say?…We found it easier than we imagined to get alongside …the atmosphere was tense before they arrived, it gradually relaxed, and ended on a happy note.'*

Some of the words of advice offered after several years of contact –

"…don't be afraid …find out what they can do, and what their interests are …pray for them… don't let whatever you do be a one-off effort – try to establish a continuity of concern."

Transport – Churches could also offer transport from the home to special activities at the church or to worship services.

A Counselling Service

A group working for **patients' and users' rights** at the national or local level.

A group working to improve **resources** at the national or local level.

Room Letting to different disabled groups can be the beginnings of friendships and contacts. A Baptist church in Milton Keynes lets its church building to a wheelchair dance group.

The 'Spinning Wheels' wheelchair dance group at Christchurch meets every Friday in the church hall. They number between 6 and 12 each week and work on routines set to both modern and classical music. They often work with young people and seek to break down the barriers between the able and disabled, offering their own abilities, friendship and enjoyment. They have performed at various city events including the opening of the City Church and the National Bowl Children's Day.

Interested? The Spinning Wheels are at your service with a ready 'Go anywhere, meet anyone' policy. They will be glad to hear from you.

Michael Cleaves

Support

We need to support those involved in professional or voluntary capacities in this area, who have responsibility in shaping the wider framework of attitudes and facilities.

Notes to leaders

1. You may like to hold this study group in the sanctuary of your church. Take a couple of wheel chairs, blindfolds and earplugs, and experience entering your church with various disabilities.

2. As well as Bibles, large sheets of paper and pens, you might contact some of the agencies listed in the resources section and get a sample of materials, either for those with learning difficulties or for those seeking to understand the issue.

3. You may wish to supplement this worksheet with a second session using the Causeway video.

1 How many people in your church are 'disabled' in some way? What is the range of disabilities? How are you defining disability?

2 If you were asked to pick up Peter, an adult with cerebral palsy, from his day centre, how would you react?

☐ No, I wouldn't know how to carry him   ☐ Great, I haven't seen Peter for a while

☐ No, I wouldn't know what to say to him   ☐ OK, but I don't want to go on my own

☐ I'd be scared of doing something wrong   ☐ Other...

3 How do we move beyond some of the negative feelings and fears?

How could the church help?

4 Read the following passages and identify any principles that help us to have a biblical approach to disability.

         1 Sam 16:7   2 Cor 12:7-10

         Isa 53:1-7   Lk 5:12f

Put your findings onto a central piece of paper.

5 Society values the strong and perfect, but has Christianity something different to offer? How can we communicate our values in this area?

6 If this young man were to move into your road, along with five other similarly disabled adults, what comments would be made? What emotions would be felt?

John Twinning

Pool your thoughts on a central piece of paper.

Belonging

7   Apart from coping with the attitudes of people, what other special pressures face the family of a severely disabled person?

8   How can the church give support to such families?

9   When you consider your church building – how would you rate it on a scale of 1-10 in terms of:

- Access to all areas ....____
- Space for wheelchairs ....____
- Toilets ....____
- Facilities for those hard of hearing..........................____
- Facilities for those with sight difficulties.................____
- Provision for those who can't read ....____

10
> A church moved its communion service from the morning to the evening because it did not want to embarrass two morning attenders who had learning difficulties. They presumably assumed that these women did not love the Lord Jesus sufficiently to share in the Supper.

- How does the church discern faith?
- What level of faith is necessary before people may receive the Lord's Supper or may become candidates for baptism and church membership?
- Has this ever been discussed in your church?
- Do you think the church referred to above chose the best course of action?

> One practical thing I resolve to do as a result of this study is .....

11   Do you have any discipleship materials for those with learning difficulties?
- If someone, unable to articulate very much, wanted to be baptised, what would you do?
- What questions would you ask?

Belonging

UNEMPLOYMENT

The experiences of being made redundant and of being unemployed often put under great strain the sense of belonging and self-worth of those involved. Unemployment can also profoundly affect the wider network of family and friends. If the person made redundant is married, it can affect the partner, the children, their home, happiness and hopes for the future. Loss of work can break up marriages, even Christian ones.

This chapter seeks to explore this theme within the social context of today and to illustrate some of the responses which churches can make.

CHANGING PATTERNS IN SOCIETY

During the 1930s the level of unemployment in Britain was very high and when Keynesian economic methods were adopted after the Second World War, one of the goals was to maintain full employment, defined so as to allow for an unemployment level of up to about 3%.

By the mid 1970s the strategy was perceived by some as having failed. The following factors were involved.

- Full employment seemed to have caused inflation.
- Industrial relations were poor.
- Nothing had succeeded in halting the decline of traditional British industries such as mining, steel making, motor manufacturing and shipbuilding. It also became apparent that cultural changes were working against the achievement of full employment; more and more women were seeking paid work and economic growth could not cope with the increased demand for employment.
- The energy crisis caused by a huge rise in the cost of oil. The net result was a high level of inflation combined with a level of unemployment (about 1 million) considered unacceptable at the time.

Today there are 2.75 million unemployed (March 1994). The most recently available statistics (*Social Trends 24* –1994) show that unemployment is highest among the young. More than 1 in 5 economically active men aged 19 and under, and nearly 1 in 6 women, were unemployed in Spring 1993.

Unemployment also varies across the country, with the highest figures in Northern Ireland, West Midlands and the North. With the exception, however, of the North, Yorkshire and Humberside, the unemployment rate increased in all regions between 1992 and 1993.

▶ What do you know about unemployment in your area? The local statistics should be available from your nearest DSS.

Redundancy rates were lower in 1993 than 1991 in all regions, but the North still has the highest redundancy rate with 1 in every 60 employees being made redundant.

Unemployment and long term unemployment is much higher amongst ethnic groups. Compared with 10% of the white population, 30% of the Pakistani/Bangladeshi and 28% of the black economically active groups are unemployed – see figures on page 100 of the Multi-cultural Community chapter.

By June 1993 there were nearly equal proportions of male and female employees. The division, however, between full-time and part-time work is marked:

	Full-time	Part-time	
Male	12,769	886	
Female	6,165	5,045	(thousands)

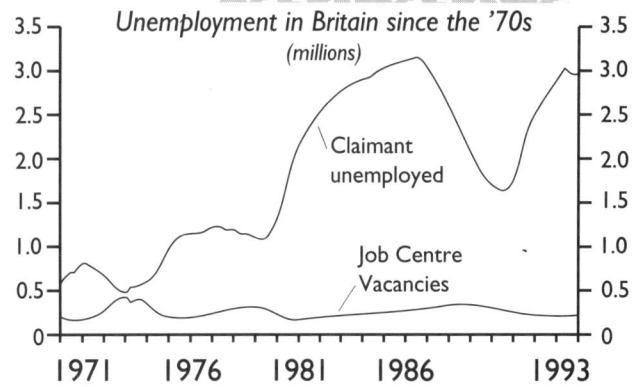

Unemployment in Britain since the '70s (millions)

BIBLICAL PERSPECTIVES

A biblical understanding of work means rejecting the simple equation between work and paid employment. Fundamental to the Bible's attitude is that work involves sharing in God's creative activity. This includes, therefore, all purposeful human activity which reflects and witnesses to God's character as creator (Gen 1:26-27; 2:8, 15). This means that whatever we do by way of service for others or activity which brings fulfilment to ourselves can be regarded as our work and done to the glory of God (1 Cor 10:31).

The Bible emphasises the positive privilege and responsibility of working for the well-being of others and for a sense of self-fulfilment. (NB It also takes seriously the inclination of human beings since the Fall to laziness.) Christians are called to witness to this broad understanding of work in a society where, contrary to scripture, work is frequently defined exclusively in terms of paid employment.

We are also called, however, to interpret the biblical material in the context of our culture where to be without paid employment brings intense feelings of alienation, low self-esteem and financial insecurity. The sense of 'belonging' in those circumstances is hard to foster.

The Christian mind is shaped in these circumstances by a biblical view which values people not because of what they 'do' but because of their inherent value to God in whose image they are made. Following from this the Bible expects that those who have been renewed in Christ will work to see justice done, will take seriously the welfare and dignity of all and will be at the forefront in practical support of all those in need. A practical strategy of generous stewardship is illustrated in the life of the early Christian community where 'selling their possessions and goods, they gave to anyone as they had need' (Acts 2:45).

THE CHURCH AND UNEMPLOYMENT

Considering Other People's Feelings

It is important for Christians to realize the changes that can take place when people lose their jobs, and to be sensitive to their feelings and needs. The emotions surrounding redundancy have been likened to those of bereavement. Work has ceased and relationships created over years come to an end. The purpose for getting up in the morning, caring for one's appearance, making an effort, can just disappear. Disbelief, anger and depression can quickly set in and take their toll on even the most resilient and optimistic believer.

Normal stress is acceptable to everybody, but abnormal stress can be caused by being out of work. Emotional symptoms can include irritability and bad temper, anxiety, irrational fear, sense of hopelessness, guilt, cynicism and self-pity. Physical symptoms can include tense muscles, dry mouth, upset stomach, nausea, diarrhoea and headaches. Behavioural symptoms can include increased smoking and drinking, nail biting, social withdrawal, reckless driving, knee jigging and finger tapping.

Counselling Christians who are stressed by this situation confirms the truth of the 'fight or flight' theory. Some will take on the situation with support from their family, faith and church fellowship and fight through to victory. Others, perhaps lacking the support they need, opt to flee. They escape into self-pity, anger at the system, negative feelings and depression. The longer they are out of work, the harder it is to climb out of the pit.

Pastoral Support for the Unemployed is a useful booklet by Julian Charley in the Grove Books series. In his section called 'Understanding the People', he gives sections on Boredom, Loss of Self-Respect and Loss of Freedom. He mentions that life can lack landmarks. One day is the same as another. If a person is not earning, she begins to feel less than a complete person and start to doubt herself. Charley states,

> *Shortage of money affects the basics of life – the food and clothing that you can afford. Holidays, once taken for granted, are now ruled out. Freedom of choice is reduced to asking, "To whom shall I be in debt this week?" It becomes a painful game of playing off one creditor against another.*

He helpfully lists a number of attitudes that Christians must guard against.

- Don't ask an unemployed person every time you meet, "Any sign of a job yet?"

- Don't treat the unemployed as if they were drop-outs or freaks.

- Don't assume that the unemployed are lazy.

> *When you are unemployed you become a pariah, as if you have a contagious disease. People don't want to talk to you and your self-esteem takes an enormous battering. What you need is comfort, support, love and reassurance, and I hadn't been aware of that before. I just thought: "Oh well, it's their own fault if they're unemployed. Let them sort it out." I can look at it a bit more compassionately now.*

Quote from Cameron Marr, a City executive who had recently experienced unemployment.

► How far does Cameron's previous attitude to out-of-work people reflect that of the people around you?

● What is your honest feeling about unemployed people?

● How can Christians display a more caring approach?

You jobless just can't imagine the stress of choosing where to go for one's winter-break holiday.

- Don't be taken in by those who say there are lots of jobs advertised at Job Centres that are not taken up.

- Don't be too quick to condemn some of the side-effects in the unemployed.

- Don't try to avoid the company of the unemployed, through fear of their making demands upon you and of your own inability to help.

There is no quick and easy answer. Every person and situation is different. However, various positive practical initiatives may be considered by the local church fellowship. This does not mean that the church has to abandon its existing programme, or start a demanding and costly ministry to the unemployed. Assistance and information do exist and there are ways the church can help its members and the community if it has a mind to do so.

Ideas for Churches

A Networking System

The diagram (based on research by British Coal Enterprise) shows that the majority of jobs are found simply by family and friends keeping their eyes and ears open for work opportunities.

A church can be a tremendous resource to those looking for jobs, simply because of the wide range of contacts represented within the fellowship. Just talking to people at church can reveal new possibilities which can be followed up. However, if a person has lost self-confidence, they may be hesitant to make such enquiries. In such a situation church members need to take sensitive initiatives, suggest ideas and pass on addresses and adverts.

A good Self-Marketing Workshop gives teaching on how to use networking and keep a check-list of those contacted, the date, telephone number, future meetings and response.

Support Groups

Prayer Triplets are not unknown to our churches. The regular meetings of three people to pray for others has been used most effectively in evangelism.

People out of work need a support group made up of fellow believers who can empathise, encourage, support in daily prayer, listen sympathetically, make suggestions and do networking, as described above. Such groups may emerge from existing house groups.

Unemployment Sunday

For many years, this has been held throughout the UK in the month of February. It is an excellent opportunity to focus the congregation's mind and spirit on the situation that pains so many in our society.

Some excellent resources for use in worship are available from agencies such as Church Action with the Unemployed, PECAN, and CHUG (for addresses see the resources chapter p144).

An interview with an unemployed church member could be an eye opener for many. Special prayers and the sharing of needs could be part of the service.

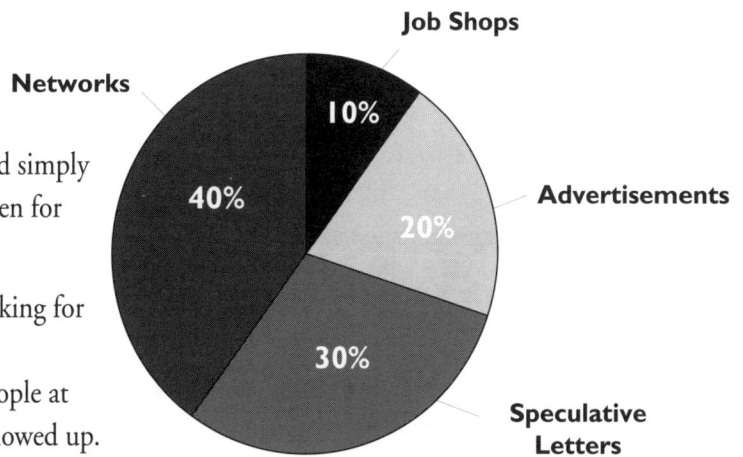

Pie chart labels: Job Shops 10%, Advertisements 20%, Speculative Letters 30%, Networks 40%

People could be encouraged, for example, to sign up for support groups, donate books of postage stamps or be a networker.

After such a service it would be good for members to spend a whole midweek evening discussing the feelings and needs of those who are out of work, and what the church could do. CHUG produces some games on unemployment that could usefully be used in groups (see p144).

Practical suggestions could be mixed with supportive prayer.

Job Search Page in the Church Magazine

In areas of high unemployment, this idea might be a practical way of helping others. One of the check-lists from the *Job Search* training materials for small groups (see page 144) could be included each time (eg, how to fill in an application form or prepare for an interview). Jobs that appear in current Christian periodicals could be included. (Many unemployed people will not be able to afford to subscribe to such periodicals.) Information about church members looking for a particular type of work could be occasionally inserted.

PRACTICAL INITIATIVES

The following initiatives can be taken by a church to support its own unemployed members, but equally, they can be offered as a service to the wider community, as the case studies illustrate.

A Self-Marketing Workshop

This could be organised and advertised by the local churches and run with outside experienced trainers, or by suitable leaders using a copy of *Jobsearch*, a special training manual for local leaders. (See page 144.)

Such a course would last a whole day and cover such points as:

- A positive mental attitude
- Preparing a good CV
- How to network
- Answering adverts correctly
- Writing speculative letters
- Preparing for the interview
- Answering hard interview questions

Most local churches have the facilities to host such a training day. You require a good size room with chairs and tables, an overhead projector and flip chart, plenty of coffee and tea and a leader with some ability in training who can follow the manual and make use of the handouts provided. (If in doubt, please contact Bryan Gilbert – 01793 871958.)

John Twinning

A Job Club

This is more ambitious and costly to organise and should only be considered if nothing is available in the locality. A job club requires regular and committed voluntary help, warm premises with tables and chairs, canteen facilities, experienced input and advice, equipment such as a photocopier, computer, word processor/electric typewriter for letters and CVs, paper, envelopes and stamps, notice-boards for adverts and information, and – if possible – a pay telephone.

Job clubs already exist in some local churches, but to make one work effectively requires costly commitment from the whole church.

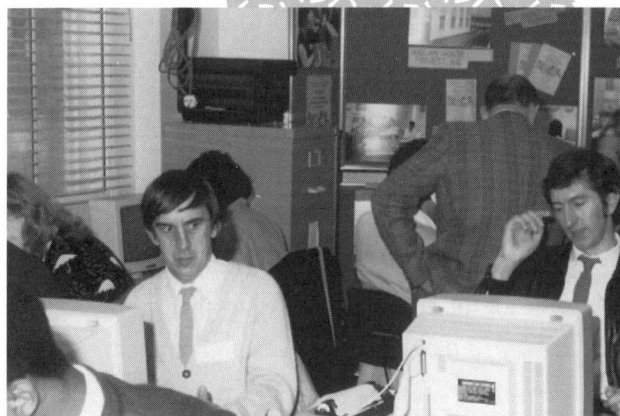

Questions the church should discuss include:

- What will be the benefits to the individual and the community?

- What premises and equipment will be needed?

- What staff requirements will be necessary, what training and who trains them?

- How will the venture be financed?

- How will the venture be advertised?

To launch such a project demands counting the cost and working out the details. Each of the above questions opens up many more questions that need to be resolved before opening a job club.

A Drop-in Meeting Place

A valuable service is a Drop-in Meeting Place, where people in similar situations can come for company, coffee and conversation, and where they are given a warm welcome and encouragement. Newspapers, current adverts, information from the Manpower Services Commission and other useful resources should be readily available. The Drop-in could provide details of opportunities such as reduced charges at sports centres, travel concessions and free further education.

A trip to the local library could be organised to uncover new targets for speculative letters.

Informal sessions to allow individuals to let off steam and vent their emotions could be organised – with care!

The group could hold a **brainstorming session** for the benefit of one of the group who is really struggling for ideas and motivation. The group could list on a flip chart or piece of paper as many suggestions as they can think of – however wild. This can provide plenty of humour, but many the gold nugget that has been unearthed!

The group could write down a list of every kind of job they see on TV during the space of one week that appeals to them. Again there will be plenty of humour in the answers, but it can provide some helpful ideas. The group could also consider creative alternatives such as self employment, combining two part-time jobs or job sharing.

Organised voluntary work can be better than sitting feeling depressed and it can sometimes open people's eyes to other types of work they may not have thought about. This could lead to applying for jobs and further education not previously considered.

Truro

Restart courses are run by training agencies who have to bid each year for the government funding that pays for the scheme, on the basis that they can provide appropriate training in suitable premises. For the last 6 years Truro Baptist Church has been able to offer a large, comfortable and well equipped seminar room at well below commercial cost.

The location, on the edge of the city centre near the railway station, is ideal. But the aspect most often commented upon by both the course members and the tutors is the atmosphere of warm and peaceful welcome. They know they are in church premises yet they don't find this at all intimidating. A significant factor in this has been the willingness of the church caretakers to go out of their way to be helpful and friendly, giving the message that the church really does care.

Unemployment is very high in Cornwall, and public resources are very limited, so when one of the church members (the chair of the local WEA group!) suggested that the church might host the Restart courses it was very much in line with the church's vision. Alongside this has been the provision of the Pottery Playgroup – the only playgroup in Truro to offer subsidised places to families in receipt of benefits. This is another obvious way of saying that the church cares about those who are unemployed.

Wallingford

The Wallingford Executive Resources Club (ERC) began in November 1992, borrowing the meeting room at Wallingford Baptist Church. This was due to the concern felt by the church at the high numbers of executives unemployed in the Wallingford area.

The church's role is to provide the premises and to offer behind-the-scenes support for individual members. Several church members do attend the club because of their own employment situation. The pastor, Revd Douglas Harbour, has several times spoken at the club and is available to offer counselling support to people from the club.

The church has very wisely steered clear of any attempt to 'preach the gospel' to the club members. It is enough of a witness that the church offers its facilities and shows that it cares. In February, an evening service was devoted to the subject of unemployment and a number of club members attended and spoke. Two unemployed Christians spoke of how their faith had helped them.

Wycliffe Baptist Church, Reading

The unemployed members of the church met initially with one of the church staff to talk about planning one or more Sunday services, focusing on the issues of loss of work. As they met to plant the morning service it became clear that meeting together and talking things over helped and supported during the difficult times of looking for work and coming to terms with the new daily activities. Meetings became ongoing and the group met each Thursday morning for an hour and a half, finishing with lunch together.

The format of the meetings was quite informal, starting with coffee. Everyone had an opportunity to 'tell their news' – of jobs they'd applied for, interviews offered/attended and letters received, while being sensitive to the fact that some may have not had any news. Members of the group passed on helpful information or handouts received from any courses they had attended connected with looking for work. Pensions, unemployment benefit, and other financial matters were other issues discussed.

A number of people in the wider fellowship of the church offered help to members of the group. Two people who worked in personnel helped with the interview techniques, putting together a good CV and career guidance; others offered casual work, for example, gardening or office work.

It was not unusual for a spouse to feel worse, more 'down' or anxious about the loss of work than the unemployed person themselves. A spin-off from the group was that a few of the wives of the unemployed men met informally occasionally to talk and pray together.

Each meeting usually closed by praying for one another; specifically for job opportunities and interviews, and generally for motivation, encouragement and perseverance.

Pecan

Pecan is an inter-church initiative working with the long-term unemployed in Peckham, South London.

In 1989, a group of churches felt the need to work together in order to tackle the problems in Peckham – particularly the chronic unemployment on the North Peckham estates that the 1980s boom years had hardly touched. Since then, it has grown to become a charity and operates a training subsidiary.

Pecan recruiters systematically visit every flat in Peckham (over 30,000 each year) and contact the most demoralised and isolated groups, inviting them personally to a free four week Employment Preparation Course. Each course has two trainers. They find out an individual's talents and interests, as well as running sessions on application forms, compiling a CV and mock interviews. Many other problems are frequently dealt with: depression, poor housing, substance abuse. For some the course is just the first step to sorting out their lives.

The approach is very effective: Pecan trained 10% of the unemployed in North Peckham last year, and two thirds have found work or gone on to appropriate vocational training.

Pecan can run seminars for churches to train members in how to help those who are out of work.

Notes to leaders

You will need to contact your local DSS office and get up-to-date statistics on unemployment in your area. Ask for as complete a breakdown of the figures as they can manage. Ask them also for material on facilities for unemployed people locally. You may find other material at the Citizens Advice Bureau. You will also need Bibles, paper and pens.

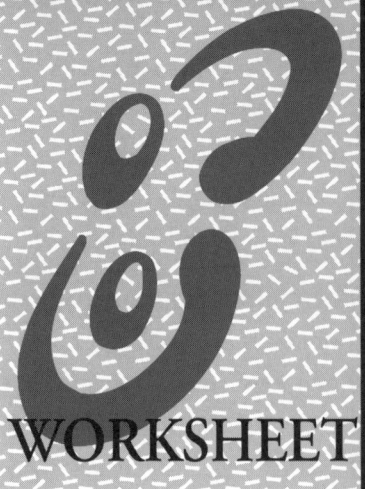

1 What would you estimate as the percentage of unemployed in your area? Do you think unemployment affects men, women and all age groups equally in your area?

Compare your guesses with the facts your leader has gathered. How do you react to the statistics?

2 What words/feelings come into your mind when you hear the word 'work'?

- ☐ Just a heavy groan
- ☐ A wave of anxiety
- ☐ It's hard to stifle a yawn
- ☐ It's a necessary evil

- ☐ A sense of satisfaction and fulfilment
- ☐ Tired but happy
- ☐ A sense of privilege
- ☐ Other...

• What do you learn about yourself from your answers?

3 Look up Genesis 1:26-27; 2:8 and 15; also Ephesians 4:28.

These verses help shape our Christian understanding of work and belonging. How?
• How would you define work?

4 Spend time identifying the varied areas of your life – paid and unpaid work, interests, leisure pursuits, other activities. List them below:

5 Which of these witness to this broad understanding of work as activity which brings fulfilment to yourself and service to others?

Belonging

6   If work is part of God's plan, is employment a basic human right, and should the church be campaigning for it?

7   Cameron Marr was made redundant from a big City firm:

When you are unemployed you become a pariah, as if you have a contagious disease. People don't want to talk to you and your self-esteem takes an enormous battering. What you need is comfort, love and reassurance, and I hadn't been aware of that. Before, I just thought: "Oh well, it's their own fault if they're unemployed. Let them sort it out." I can look at it a bit more compassionately now.

Can you list some other feelings experienced by unemployed people?

8   Sometimes people say that there are always jobs advertised in their local papers so they can't understand why people aren't working. What other attitudes do you hear expressed about unemployed people?

● How do you respond to these?

9   How should the church be responding to the high unemployment figures?

● What can churches do?

10   What facilities for unemployed people already exist in your area? Are they sufficient?

● How would you find out?
● Are there ways you could get involved in these?

One practical thing I resolve to do as a result of this study is .....

11   Imagine your church had been asked to start up a Drop-in Centre for unemployed people. What questions would you need to answer before it would go ahead?

Belonging

Worship Resources

Many of the resources on the following pages are interchangeable. However a rough guide is offered on this page to those resources which are especially relevant to certain chapter headings.

Giving Thanks for Families

The response at the end of each sentence is: *We give you thanks, and praise your holy name.*

We give thanks for God's gifts we discern in families around us:

We thank you for the resilience we see in families, for the courage and resourcefulness of people under pressure, and their love which outweighs all hurts.

We thank you for family caring which bridges generations, for all who can be relied on to be there for those who need them, and the selflessness of their love.

We thank you for the joy which shines through loving families even in adversity, for the light in children's eyes, and the inner happiness of knowing we are loved.

We thank you for the sense of belonging within the family, for the trust and peace that comes from being accepted as we are.

We thank you for the opportunities for growth which family life brings, for all the learning from each other that leads to fuller and richer life.

From the National Ecumenical Service of Dedication for the UN International Year of the Family 1994

Praying for Families

A candle is lit in the silence after each sentence, and then the response is: *We pray your light may shine, and bring healing and hope.*

In confidence that God's love surrounds all creation, we bring our prayers for families facing difficulties, and light a candle to represent our loving concern.

We pray for families who are homeless, for those who are overcrowded, for those who feel insecure.

We pray for families who face illness and pain, for those who see people they love suffering, and who feel helpless.

We pray for families facing loss and separation, through deprivation, disagreement and division, divorce or death: who live with the constant ache of someone not being present, or who feel rejected.

We pray for families coping with long-term disability: for the young learning to handle everyday living, for adults for whom life is strenuous, for elderly people, learning to live with declining powers, and for all who feel life is limited.

We pray for families who have come to the end of their resources, and now feel hopeless and despairing: for all who feel vulnerable and alone.

(From NESoD for UNIYF 1994)

Dedication of Families to Christ

The five candles lit in 'Praying for Families' are handed to representatives of five families.

Take the light of Christ into your home, and with it the gift of God's presence, to give you resilience in all you face together.

Take the light of Christ into your home, and with it the gift of God's love, to inspire you in all your mutual caring.

Take the light of Christ into your home, and with it the gift of God's grace, to fill your hearts with the joy of our Lord.

Take the light of Christ into your home, and with it the gift of God's peace, to give you confidence that you belong to him for ever.

Take the light of Christ into your home, and with it the gift of God's life, that you may grow in love all the days of your life.

All: May we all know these gifts of God in every family represented here. We dedicate ourselves to bring the light of Christ into all our relationships, and to share God's gifts wherever we go.

(From NESoD for UNIYF 1994)

Collect for the Church

O God, who has called us in Christ to be members of your family, the Church: give us such love towards each other that the world may see in our common life a reflection of your love for us all. Through Jesus Christ our Lord. Amen.

Praying for Society

When the leader says: *Help us to show your love,* the response is: ***By the way we treat each other.***

We pray for those who are despised for any reason, for those who offend against society's codes, those who do not fit in, those with whom we find it hard to sympathise.
Help us to show your love…

We pray for those who look down on us, and who make us feel inadequate or unwanted.
Help us to show your love…

We pray for those who do the menial tasks, at home, at work, and in the places where we take our leisure. May we appreciate how much we need them.
Help us to show your love…

We pray for our fellow-Christians, especially those with whom we find it difficult to see eye to eye.
Help us to show your love…

We pray for all who make us irritable, or provoke us to behave in ways we later regret.
Help us to show your love…

From FLAME 1994, IYF

Hymn: *The Barriers that Part Us*

The barriers that part us by Christ have been broken:
not colour, nor gender, nor class must divide.
Opinions and natures may clash and bring tension,
but all stand rebuked by the cross where he died.

So we must put on, as God's cherished and chosen,
the clothing of Christians, the garments of grace:
be humble and gentle, with hearts of compassion,
be kind and be patient, to others give place.

Rejoicing in differences, bearing with failings,
as Christ has forgiven, so let us forgive,
and putting on love, as the crown and completion,
together in unity learn how to live.

For God who made us counts each of us precious,
and Christ lives within us, in you and me.
To peace we are called, and his peace must control us,
for none but his servants can truly be free.

Stella Read, Bristol

Based on Col 3:11-15
Tune: The Ash Grove

A Creed from Indonesia

All   I believe in God, who is love and who has given the earth to all people.
I believe in Jesus Christ, who came to heal us, and to free us from all forms of oppression.
I believe in the Spirit of God, who works in and through all who are turned towards the truth.
I believe in the Community of faith, which is called to be at the service of all people.
I believe in God's promise to finally destroy the power of sin in us all, and to establish the Kingdom of justice and peace of all humankind.

Gp A   I do not believe in the right of the strongest, nor the force of arms, nor the power of oppression.

Gp B   I believe in human rights, in the solidarity of all people, in the power of non-violence.

Gp A   I do not believe in racism, in the power that comes from wealth and privilege, or in any established order that enslaves.

Gp B   I believe that all men and women are equally human, that order based on violence and injustice is not order.

Gp A   I do not believe that war and hunger are inevitable and peace unattainable.

Gp B   I believe in the beauty of simplicity, in love with open hands, in peace on earth.

Gp A   I do not believe that suffering need be in vain, that death is the end, that the disfigurement of our world is what God intended.

All   But I dare to believe, always and in spite of everything, in God's power to transform and transfigure, fulfilling his promise of a new heaven and a new earth where justice and peace will flourish.

Family Spirit – a Festival Service for Pentecost

CALL TO WORSHIP

Leader: This is the day which the Lord has made.
Response: **We will rejoice and be glad in it.**
This is the day when the Spirit came.
We will rejoice and be glad in it.

Hymn Creator Spirit, by whose aid
Baptist Praise & Worship 286

Prayer Almighty God, to whom all hearts are …
Patterns & Prayers for Christian Worship p30

Dramatic Reading Acts 2:1-41

Prayer Exuberant Spirit of God … we praise you
Bread of Tomorrow p145

Notices and offering

> **Offertory Prayer**
>
> Heavenly Father, through the Holy Spirit you pour out your love on your world. We offer our gifts, our lives, our praise in celebration of your coming.

THE WORD OF GOD

Hymn

Holy Spirit, truth divine
(*BPW* 292)

Reading

Galatians 4:1-7 (GNB)

Sermon

'Family Spirit' – *Spirit of freedom to trust God, to grow together, to give to the world*

MEDITATION
Prayer of Thanksgiving

Hymn

I come with joy to meet my Lord (*Praise for Today* 40)

This originally appeared in *Partners in Learning* 1992 and used material from Iona. At the end of each section of the meditation, an appropriate object was laid on the table at the front of the church.

After each 'Age' there is a sung response as follows

Where there is love and tender care,
Where there is love, God indeed is there (*sung to Ubi Caritas, Taizé*)

Babyhood *Psalm 139:13, 15, 16a*	Before I was born, you prayed for me; and when I moved from the womb to the world, your arms cradled me; and you sang your funny songs, and understood my wordless language, held my hand till I slept, till I walked, till I lost my fear, till I was old enough to let your hand go.	Where there is love…
Childhood *Luke 2:46-48*	Reflections on the nurture and constraints.	Where there is love…
Youth *1 Timothy 4:7, 8, 12*	Reflections on the tensions and opportunities felt by a young person.	Where there is love…
Adulthood *Philippians 4:10a, 14, 15b, 18d*	Reflections on the experiences of a grown-up	Where there is love…

COMMUNION

Voice 1	When we bless the cup of blessing is it not a means of sharing in the blood of Christ?
Voice 2	When we break the bread is it not a means of sharing in the body of Christ?
Voice 3	Because there is one loaf, we, many as we are, are one body for it is one loaf of which we all partake.
Voice 2	We are your family Lord. In your family each of us has a part to play, from the youngest to the oldest. In your family we must care for each other, encourage each other, pray for each other, forgive each other and love each other.
Voice 1	This body, this blood, this bread, this wine, for the living heart of faith for your family.
Voice 3	From this communion come love and hope. From this communion come forgiveness and peace.
Voice 2	From this communion come healing and strength From this communion comes life … that never ends.
Voice 3	Thank you Lord that these, your gifts, are for each of us. Help us to share them freely with each other as your family,
Voice 1	So that together we can work to share them with the world.

Presentation of the Bread and Wine

Lord's Prayer

Holy Communion

Prayers of Intercession

- For the family of the local church.
- For the world-wide church.
- For families around the world.
- For the whole life together of the planet.

Hymn There's a spirit in the air (*BPW* 300)

Blessing Go into God's world…(*PPCW* p90)

> *This service was planned by David Wilcox and Junior Church leaders at their church. The idea was to take the theme of 'Family', church, home and human, and joyfully affirm the Spirit's involvement in all areas. Children were actively involved in the dramatic reading, with adults in the meditation, and in the presentation.*

Anniversary Affirmation

WE the members and friends of .... Baptist Church believe that God has called us to be his people in this place, in partnership with other Christians in our neighbourhood and with the wider church.

WE believe that we have been called to share in God's mission in his world, through evangelism, friendship and caring, prophetic witness and prayer.

This is God's work and we seek his help in fulfilling it.

WE offer to God our life together that our fellowship might be:

a place where we bear each other's burdens and share each other's joys;

a place where we are each enabled to grow in our love of the Lord Jesus Christ and in our knowledge of God.

WE are brothers and sisters in Christ and we rejoice in the diversity of experience and gifts that we bring one to another. We affirm that the church fellowship is a place where all are valued and encouraged to receive and to give – young and old, black and white, rich and poor, strong and weak.

WE are thankful for the opportunities which have been entrusted to us through this building.

WE commit ourselves to using our resources for the building up of fellowship, the service of the neighbourhood and the benefit of the wider church.

All these things we offer to God – what we have and what we are.

WE confess that we fall short of this vision but ask God for his forgiveness and help, that he might do his will through us. We praise him for his faithfulness and for the vision that he gives us, we pray that his Spirit will enable us to be faithful and loving in all we do; in the name of Christ. Amen.

Beatitudes of the Disabled

Blessed are you who take time to listen to defective speech, for you help us to know that if we persevere we can be understood.

Blessed are you who walk with us in public places and ignore the stares of strangers, for in your companionship we find havens of relaxation.

Blessed are you that never bid us "hurry up" and more blessed are you that do not snatch our tasks from our hands to do them for us, for often we need time rather than help.

Blessed are you that stand beside us as we enter new untried ventures, for our failures will be out-weighed by the times we surprise ourselves and you.

Blessed are you who ask for our help, for our greatest need is to be needed.

Blessed are you when by all these things you assure us that the things which make us individuals is not our peculiar muscles, nor our wounded nervous systems, but is the God-given self that no infirmity can confine.

Rejoice and be exceedingly glad, and know that you give us reassurances that cannot be spoken in words, for you deal with us as Christ dealt with handicapped people.

A Prayer on Sunday night

Tonight, Lord, I am alone.
Little by little the sounds died down in the church,
The people went away,
And I came home,
Alone.

I passed the people who were returning from a walk.
I went by the cinema that was disgorging its crowd.
I skirted the café terraces where tired strollers were
trying to prolong the pleasure of a Sunday holiday.
I bumped into youngsters playing on the footpath,
Youngsters, Lord,
Other people's youngsters who will never be my own.

Here I am, Lord,
Alone.
The silence troubles me,
The solitude oppresses me.

Lord, I'm 35 years old,
A body made like others,
ready for work,
A heart meant for love,
But I've given you all.
It's true, of course, that you needed it.
I've given you all, but it's hard, Lord.
It's hard to give one's body; it would like to give itself to
others.
It's hard to love everyone and to claim no one.
It's hard to shake a hand and not want to retain it.
It's hard to inspire affection, to give it to you.
It's hard to be nothing to oneself in order to be
everything to others.
It's hard to be like others, among others, and to be of
them.
It's hard always to give without trying to receive.
It's hard to seek out others and to be unsought oneself.
It's hard to suffer from the sins of others, and yet be
obliged to hear and bear them.

It's hard to be told secrets, and be unable to share them.
It's hard to carry others and never, even for a moment,
be carried.
It's hard to sustain the feeble and never be able to lean
on one who is strong.

It's hard to be alone,
Alone before everyone,
Alone before the world,
Alone before suffering,
death,
sin.

Son, you are not alone,
I am with you,
I am you.
For I needed another human vehicle to continue my
Incarnation and my Redemption.
Out of all eternity, I chose you,
I need you.

I need your hands to continue to bless,
I need your lips to continue to speak,
I need your body to continue to suffer,
I need your heart to continue to love,
I need you to continue to save,
Stay with me, son.

Here I am, Lord;
Here is my body,
Here is my heart,
Here is my soul.
Grant that I may be big enough to reach the world,
Strong enough to carry it,
Pure enough to embrace it without wanting to keep it.
Grant that I may be a meeting-place, but a temporary
one,
A road that does not end in itself, because everything to
be gathered there, everything human, leads toward you.

Lord, tonight, while all is still and I feel sharply the sting
of solitude,
While men devour my soul and I feel incapable of
satisfying their hunger,
While the whole world presses on my shoulders with all
its weight of misery and sin,
I repeat to you my "yes" – not in a burst of laughter,
but slowly, clearly, humbly,
Alone, Lord, before you,
In the peace of the evening.

Michel Quoist

Praying about Marriage

After each sentence, the person leading the prayer says: *Spirit of God.*
The congregation responds: ***Guide and bless them.***

We pray for all those who have recently married, as they settle into their new way of life.

We pray for all who are preparing for marriage, and for the families from which they come.

We pray for all who help with marriage preparation schemes.

We pray for all who provide marriage support and marriage enrichment courses.

We pray for FLAME, the Mothers' Union, and all who encourage marriage education.

We pray for all whose marriages are under stress.

We pray for Relate, and all who counsel people with marriage problems.

We pray for those who mourn the end of a marriage, through death or divorce.

Wedding Prayer

Heavenly Father, we thank you
that our human love for one another
is the gift – and a taste –
of your divine love for us.
As we rejoice now with ......and ......,
celebrating their love
and witnessing their commitment,
we pray for your blessing on their marriage.
As the years go by
and their relationship deepens
and changes,
may they find in it
not only the reassurance of constancy
but also the stimulus of continual discovery
and surprise;
may they find in one another
both their belonging
and their freedom.
Let each possess the other
not as an owner but as a friend;
let each explore the other
not as an intruder but as a guest;
let each submit to the other
not in duty but in love
through the grace
of our Lord Jesus Christ.

Jamie Wallace, Northampton

Ten Beatitudes for Parents

Blessed are the parents who can laugh at themselves, for their children will laugh with them and not at them.

Blessed are those who can see the world with the freshness and excitement of a small child, for they will always be young in heart.

Blessed are the parents of babies who can wake up joyful and clear of eye at 5.45am, for they will have to get up at that hour anyway.

Blessed are they who spend adequate time caring for their children during infancy and childhood, for they shall be spared many teenage problems.

Blessed are the parents who let their children do for themselves whatever they are capable of doing, for they shall not be merely unpaid servants.

Blessed are the parents who take their children with them often, for they shall see the world with fresh eyes.

Blessed are the fathers and mothers who spend time together occasionally without their offspring, for they shall not go stark crazy.

Blesssed are they who listen to their children, for they in turn will be heard.

Blessed are they who can be a warm fire of encouragement for their children, for their offspring will not stay away long from a hearth where they can warm their soul.

Blessed are they who enjoy their children, for they have found a new dimension of love and a reward for their efforts.

From a course run by the Family Life Project of Lichfield Diocese

My Parents

Sunday is a funny day,
It starts with lots of noise.
Mummy rushes round with socks,
And daddy shouts: "You boys!"

Then mummy says: "Now don't blame them,
You know you're just as bad,
You've only just got out of bed,
It really makes me mad."

My mummy is a Christian,
My daddy is as well,
My mummy says: "Oh heavens!"
My daddy says: "Oh, hell!"

And when we get to church at last,
It's really very strange,
'Cos mum and dad stop arguing,
And suddenly they change.

At church my mum and dad are friends,
They get on very well,
But no one knows they've had a row,
And I'm not gonna tell.

People often come to them,
Because they seem so nice,
And mum and dad are very pleased
To give them some advice.

They tell them Christian freedom
Is worth an awful lot,
But I don't know what freedom means,
If freedom's what they've got.

I once heard my mummy say
She'd walk out of his life.
I once heard daddy say to her
He'd picked a rotten wife.

They really love each other
I really think they do.
I think the people in the church
Would help them – if they knew.

Adrian Plass

Call to Worship
by Child and Leader

Child: What is the meaning of this?
Why is there bread and wine on the table today?

Leader: Jesus told us to remember him in this way

All: And this has been done from the earliest days of the church until now.

Child: I don't understand.
How do bread and wine remind us of Jesus?

Leader: Jesus said, "This bread is like my body – broken when I died for you."
"This wine is like my blood – spilt when I died for you."

Child: Is Jesus dead, then?

Leader: No, he came alive again and promises to be among us when we all meet in his name.

All: Christ has died; Christ is risen; Christ will come again.

Child: So Jesus is here. Lord Jesus we welcome you to this place today.

Michael Hambleton, Abingdon

Illustration

Your children are not your children.
They are the sons and daughters of Life's longing for itself.
They come through you but not from you,
And though they are with you yet they belong not to you.
You may give them your love but not your thoughts,
For they have their own thoughts.
You may house their bodies but not their souls,
For their souls dwell in the house of tomorrow,
which you cannot visit, not even in your dreams.
For life goes not backward nor tarries with yesterday.
You are the bows from which your children as living arrows are sent forth.
The Archer sees the mark upon the path of the infinite, and He bends you
with His might that His arrows may go swift and far.
Let your bending in the Archer's hand be for gladness;
For even as He loves the arrow that flies, so He loves also the bow that is stable.

from *The Prophet* by Kahill Gibran

A Prayer for Children – from the USA

We pray for children who sneak biscuits from the tin before supper, for those who make a mess of their school books, who can never find their shoes.

And we pray for those who have no shoes, no biscuits to sneak, no books to read, who stare at photographers from behind fences, who are born in places we would never enter, who live in an X-rated world.

We pray for children who bring in sticky kisses and fists full of dandelions, who hug us in a hurry, and forget their lunch money.

And we pray for those who never get a kiss, who walk on wasteland, who watch their parents watch them die, who can't find any bread, whose pictures are on nobody's wall, whose monsters are real.

We pray for children who spend all their pocket money in one day, who throw tantrums in the supermarket, who pick at their food, who scream in the telephone, who shove dirty clothes under their beds, who get visits from the tooth fairy, who squirm in church.

And we pray for those whose nightmares come in the daytime, who have never seen a dentist, who cannot talk to anyone, who are not spoilt by anyone, who go to bed hungry and cry themselves to sleep. They live and move but have no being.

We pray for children who want to be carried and for children who must; for those we never give up on and for those who never get a second chance. We pray for those whom we spoil and for those who are looking for anybody's hand to take.

Lord Jesus, you love children, we pray that will not hinder them, but that we may do all that we can to let them come to you. We cannot bring every child into your presence, but we can bring so many.

137

Prayer of a 17ᵗʰ Century Nun

Lord, thou knowest better than I know myself that I am growing older and will someday be old. Keep me from the fatal habit of thinking that I must say something on every subject and on every occasion. Release me from craving to straighten out everybody's affairs. Make me thoughtful but not moody; helpful, but not bossy. With my vast store of wisdom, it seems a pity not to use it all, but thou knowest, Lord, that I want a few friends at the end.

Keep my mind free from the recital of endless details; give me wings to get to the point. Seal my lips on my aches and pains. They are increasing, and love of rehearsing them is becoming sweeter as the years go by. I dare not ask for grace enough to enjoy the tales of others' pains, but help me to endure them with patience.

I dare not ask for improved memory, but for a growing humility and a lessening cocksureness when my memory seems to clash with the memories of others. Teach me the glorious lesson that occasionally I may be mistaken.

Keep me reasonably sweet; I do not want to be a Saint – some of them are so hard to live with – but a sour old person is one of the crowning works of the devil. Give me the ability to see good things in unexpected places, and talents in unexpected people. And give me, O Lord, the grace to tell them so.

Amen.

Creed for the Unemployed

We believe in God, the worker,
who created men and women
in His own image.
We believe that people are born
to lead fulfilling, creative and
productive lives.
We believe that unemployment
and frustrating work
are a denial of God's image in us.
We believe that in the church
God is creating a community of people
who care for each other,
bear one another's burdens
and reach out to the wider world
with the good news of God
who cares and creates
and is building his Kingdom
today.

From a pack produced by PECAN

Responsive Prayer

Leader: Lord we come to you with our feelings of helplessness and concern about the unemployed.

Response: Lord hear us as we come to you.

Leader: We come with our desire to help and to offer support.

Response: Lord hear us as we come to you.

Leader: Show us how, with our strength and resources, we can empower those without work.

Response: Lord hear us as we come to you.

Leader: Show us how, with our love and support, we can comfort those without work.

Response: Lord hear us as we come to you.

Leader: Show us how we can help those without work to open doors back into the world of work.

Response: Lord hear us as we come to you, and help us, by your powerful Spirit, to turn words into actions for the sake of Jesus Christ, our Lord. Amen.

Resources

The following list of further resources suggests, chapter by chapter, both reading/study material and agencies offering specialist advice, training and support.

First, a general list gives details of organisations and agencies which offer resources and/or training relating to several or all the themes covered in the book.

GENERAL

Family Policy Studies Centre
(produces excellent background material on the family)

231 Baker Street
London NW1 6XE
Tel: 0171 486 8211

Family Welfare Association

501-505 Kingsland Road
London E8 4AU
Tel: 0171 254 6251

Christian Family Concern
(adoption agency; residential family support and assessment centre)

42 South Hill Park Road
Croydon
Surrey CR2 7YB
Tel: 0181 688 0251

CARE Trust
(Christian Action
Research and Education)
(supporting Christian standards in society
and co-ordinating practical initiatives)

53 Romney Street
London SW1P 3PF
Tel: 0171 233 0455

Scripture Union Training Unit
(consultancy to churches and
organisations on training.
Runs a Family Work consultancy
and training programme)

The Family Work
Co-ordinator
SU Training Unit
26-30 Heathcoat Street
Nottingham NG1 3AA
Tel: 0115 941 4624

Bible Society

Stonehill Green
Westlea
Swindon
Wiltshire SN5 7D6
Tel: 01793 513713

Evangelical Alliance

Whitefield House
186 Kennington Park Road
London SE11 4BT
Tel: 0171 582 0228

BELONGING AND SOCIETY

Derek Tidball, *Catching the Tide* (Baptist Union, 1991)

Alvin Toffler, *Future Shock*

Tony Walter, *A Long Way From Home* (Paternoster Press, 1979)
Love in Action (Shaftesbury Society, 1991)

Social Trends 24 – 1994 Edition (HMSO, 1994)

Greg Smith
(community surveys)

Community Involvement
Unit
Durning Hall
Earlham Grove
London
E7 9AB

Christian Impact
(helping Christians relate
their faith to every area of
their responsibility)

St Peter's Church
Vere Street
London W1M 9HP
Tel: 0171 629 3615

Jubilee Trust
(research and campaigning
organisation – seeking to
bring Christian values to
bear on public policy)

Jubilee House
3 Hooper Street
Cambridge CB1 2NZ
Tel: 01223 311596

FAMILY VALUES

Stephen Barton, 'Towards a Theology of the Family' in *Crucible* (Quarterly Journal of the Anglican Board of Social Responsibility) January-March 1993 (published by Church House Publishing)

Dietrich Bonhoeffer, *Life Together* (SCM)

Anne Borrowdale, *Reconstructing Family Values* (SPCK, July 1994)

Michael Moynagh, *Home to Home* (Daybreak, 1990)

What is the Future of the Family? (Church of England Board of Social Responsibility, Church House Publishing)

International Year of the Family (Family Life Education Ecumenical Project; c/o Free Church Federal Council, 27 Tavistock Street, London WC1H 9HH)

COMMUNITY LIVING

David Gillett, Anne Long and Ruth Fowke, *A Place in the Family* (Grove Books, Nottingham, 1893)

Jeanne Hinton, *Communities* (Eagle)

Paul Tournier, *The Strong and the Weak* (SCM)

Jean Vanier, *Community and Growth* (DLT)

Richard Foster, *Celebration of Discipline* (Hodder and Stoughton, 1989)

Richard Foster, *Freedom of Simplicity* (Triangle/SPCK, 1981)

Michael Schluter and Roy Clements, *Reactivating the Extended Family* (Jubilee Centre Paper No 1; 1986)

National Association of Christian Communities and Networks (NACCAN) (sharing the vision of Christian community with churches and society)	1046 Bristol Road Selly Oak Birmingham West Midlands B29 6LJ Tel: 0121 472 8079
Netherspring Trust	Roy Searle Cheviot House Cheviot Street Wooler Northumberland NE71 6LN Tel: 01668 81069

SINGLENESS

Steve Chilcraft, *One of Us* – single people as part of the church (Word, 1993)

Margaret Clarkson, *Single* (Kingsway, 1980)

Margaret Evening, *Who Walk Alone* (Hodder and Stoughton, 1974)

David Gillett, Anne Long, Ruth Fowke, *A Place in the Family* (Grove Books, Nottingham, 1987)

Donald Goergen, *The Sexual Celibate* (SPCK, 1976)

Elizabeth-Ann Horsford, *Complete as One* (CARE)

Roger Hurding, *Restoring the Image* (Paternoster, 1980)

Ada Lum, *Single and Human* (IVP)

Henri Nouwen, *Reaching Out* (Collins, 1976)

John Powell, *Why am I afraid to Love?* (Fontana)

One Plus (ministry to single people)	Elizabeth-Ann Horsford c/o Hildenborough Trust Townsend Chambers Amherst Hill Sevenoaks Kent TN13 3DS Tel: 01732 460625
Singularly Significant	Evangelical Alliance Whitefield House 186 Kennington Park Road London SE11 4BT Tel: 071 582 6221 Tel: 01491 8731952

MARRIAGE

An Honourable Estate (Church House Publishing, 1988)

Jack Dominion, *Make or Break – an introduction to marriage counselling* (1984)

Kathleen Fischer and Thomas Hart, *Promises to Keep: Developing the Skills of Marriage* (Triangle/SPCK, 1993)

Richard Foster, *Money, Sex and Power* (Hodder and Stoughton, 1985)

A Thatcher, *Liberating Sex – a Christian sexual theology* (SPCK, 1993)

K Scott and M Warren, *Perspectives on Marriage: a Reader* (OUP, 1993)

S Walrond-Skinner, *The Fulcrum and the Fire* (DLT, 1993)

S Walrond-Skinner, *Family Matters* (SPCK, 1988)

Married Listening Programme – A boxed kit (Family Caring Trust)

Marriage Matters – with Rob and Dianne Parsons (CARE – see below for details)

Marriage in Mind – videos for use in marriage preparation and enrichment are available from Church Pastoral Aid Society, Athena Drive, Tatchbrook Park, Warwick CV34 6NG. Tel: 01926 334242.

Relate (formerly National Marriage Guidance Council)	Herbert Gray College Little Church Street Rugby CV21 3AP Tel: 01788 73241 see telephone book for local branches)
Association for Marriage Enrichment (enabling couples to communicate more effectively, understand each other better and achieve greater intimacy)	Westminster Pastoral Foundation 23 Kensington Square London W8 5HN Tel: 0171 937 6956

CARE
(providing support for marriages through seminars and resources)

53 Romney Street
London SWlP 3RF
Tel: 0171 233 0455

Marriage Encounter - Baptist Expression
(encouraging married couples to strengthen and deepen their relationship with each other)

12 South Street
Leighton Buzzard
Bedfordshire
LU7 8NT
Tel: 01525 371312

Men, Women and God
(education and research in changing roles, relationships and ministries of women in church and society)

St Peter's Church
Vere Street
London WlM 9HP
Tel: 0171 629 3615

Marriage Review
(residential weekend courses for married couples and non-residential courses for churches)

6 Wilton Drive
Collier Row
Romford
Essex RM5 3TJ
Tel: 01708 742907

Family Alive!
(residential weekends and local church seminars for couples, strengthening communication and intimacy in marriage)

4 Temple Row
Birmingham
West Midlands
B2 5HG
Tel: 0121 333 3677

DIVORCE

Christopher Compston, *Recovering from Divorce* (Hodder and Stoughton, 1993)

Andrew Cornes, *Divorce and Re-marriage*

Robert Warren, *Divorce and Re-marriage* (Grove Books, Nottingham)

Divorce Recovery Workshop

6 Hever Close
Maidenhead Berks
SL6 4RH
Tel: 01628 773292

Network of Access and Child Contact Centres
(for children of separated families)

St Andrew's with
Castlegate URC
Goldsmith Street
Nottingham NG1 5JT
Tel: 0115 948 4557

National Council for the Divorced and Separated

13 High Street
Little Shelford
Cambridge
CB2 5ES
Tel: 01533 708880

Rebuilders Ministry
(a ministry for marital restoration and divorce recovery)

Willow Creek Assoc
PO Box 3188
Barrington
Illinois 60011-3188
USA

PARENTING

James Dobson, *Dare to Discipline*

James Dobson, *Discipline While You Can*

What Can A Parent Do? (1987)
The Teen Parenting Programme – Two kits with cassettes, posters, leaders and participants guides from Family Caring Trust (see details below)

Partners in Parenting – discussion starters (Methodist Division of Education and Youth, 1993)

Parenting for Peace and Justice (McGinnis Herald Press)

Parentwise — a monthly magazine for parents. Available from Elm House Christian Communications Ltd., 37 Elm Road, New Malden, Surrey KT3 3HB. Tel: 0181 942 9761.

Tapewise (details below) offer a series of Tapes For Parents. Each pack consists of a 60 minute audio tape and a booklet. Themes covered: Teenagers and Sexuality; Teenagers in the Family; Teenagers Under Stress.

Family Caring Trust

44 Rathfriland Road,
Newry
Co Down BT34 1LD
Tel: 01693 64174

Exploring Parenthood

Latimer Education Centre
194 Freston Road
London W10 6TT

Spurgeon's Child Care

74 Wellingborough Road
Rushden
Northants NN10 9TY
Tel: 01933 412412

Tapewise

23 New Road
Brighton
East Sussex BN1 1WZ
Tel: 01273 680281

Bodey House
(West Ham Central Mission's counselling ministry to families)

Stock Road
Stock
Ingatestone Essex
CM4 9DH
Tel: 01277 840668

Adventures in Parenting
(activity based courses to enable parents and children to have time together)

CARE Trust
53 Romney Street
London SWlP 3RF
Tel: 0171 233 0455

Care for the Family
(support for families through seminars, resources, special projects and correspondence)

CARE Trust (as above)

National Council for One Parent Families

255 Kentish Town
London NW5 2LX
Tel: 0171 267 1361

Christian Link Association of Single Parents (CLASP)

Linden
Shorter Avenue
Shenfield Brentwood
Essex CM15 8RE
Tel: 01277 233848

Single Parent Travel Club

37 Sunningdale Park
Queen Victoria Road
New Tupton
Chesterfield S42 6DZ
Tel: 01246 865069

Network of Access and Child Contact Centres (NACCC)

(co-ordinating body for local child contact centres)

St Andrew's with
Castle Gate URC
Goldsmith Street
Nottingham NG1 5JT
Tel: 0115 948 4557

CHILDREN

Francis Bridger, *Children Finding Faith* (Scripture Union, 1988)

Ron Buckland, *Children and God* (Scripture Union)

Paul Butler, *Reaching Children* (Scripture Union)

Richard Cole, *The Spiritual Life Of Children*

Peter Graystone and Eileen Turner, *A Church for All Ages* (Scripture Union)

John Westerhoff, *Will Our Children Have Faith?* (Seabury Press, 1976)

Children in the Way – A report for the General Synod of the Church of England (Church House Publishing)

All God's Children? (Church House Publishing)

Being a Church Family Together – Resources for training leaders and preparing a church for being a relating community in which children are welcome. The pack also contains learning and worship materials for use with all ages together i.e. activities to enable a sense of belonging in churches. Available from Scripture Union Training Unit in mid-1994.

Children's Society

Edward Rudolf House
Margery Street
London WC1X OJL
Tel: 0171 837 4299

Spurgeon's Child Care

30 Mill Street
Bedford MK40 3HD
Tel: 01234 261843

Children's Family Trust
(providing a lasting family background for children unable to return to their own families)

Maracas
Church Road
Farnham Royal
Slough
Berks SL2 3AW
Tel: 01753 642137

Christian Child Care Network
(a network of Christian individuals, families and organisations caring for children)

10 Crescent Road
South Woodford
London E18 lJ
Tel: 0181 559 1133

YOUNG PEOPLE

Nick Atkin, *Creative Ideas for Youth Evangelism* (Marshall Pickering, 1992)

Mike Breen, *Outside In* (Scripture Union, 1993)

Peter Brierley, *Reaching and Keeping Teenagers* (Monarch, 1993)

Tony Campolo, *Ideas for Social Action* (Youth Specialities, 1991)

Pete Gilbert, *Understanding Teenagers* (Crossway Books)

Roger Hurding, *Understanding Adolescence* (Kingsway, 1989)

Patricia Noller and Victor Callan, *The Adolescent in the Family* (Routledge, 1991)

Lance Pierson, *The Pastoral Care of Young People* (Grove Books)

William J Rowley, *Equipped to Care* (Victor Books, 1990)

Peter Ward, *Worship and Youth Culture* (Marshall Pickering, 1993)

Peter Ward, *Youth Culture and the Gospel* (Marshall Pickering, 1993)

Youth Worker Magazine, (published bi-monthly by Elm House Publishing)

Baptist Youth Ministry
(encouraging and stimulating churches to be effective in their work with young people)

Baptist Union of Great Britain
Mission Department
Baptist House
129 Broadway
Didcot Oxon OX11 8RT
Tel: 01235 512077

Frontier Youth Trust
(associating, servicing and training Christians working with disadvantaged young people in urban/industrial missionary areas)

Scripture Union House
130 City Road
London EC1V 2NJ
Tel: 0171 250 1966

Band of Hope Union
(alcohol and other drugs education for children, young people, parents, leaders, teachers)

25f Copperfield Street
London SE1 OEN
Tel: 0171 928 0848

Church Pastoral Aid Society

Athena Drive
Tachbrook Park
Warwick CV34 6NG

National Youth Agency

17-23 Albion Street
Leicester LE1 6GD

Scripture Union in Schools
(fostering voluntary Christian groups in schools in England and Wales and running residential activities)

130 City Road
London EClV 2NJ
Tel: 0171 782 0013

OLDER PEOPLE

Michael Botting, *Christians in Retirement* (Grove Books, Nottingham, 1986)

Arthur Greber, *New Approaches to Ministry with Older People* (Grove Books, Nottingham)

Donald Rutherford, *A View From the Hill* (Souvenir Press, 1987)

Don Black, *Seniors* (Baptist Union)

Plus (Quarterly Journal of the Christian Council on Ageing)

Tape recordings of Bible readings, together with large print Bibles and books, available from Torch Trust (see under Disability section)

Christian Council on Ageing

Caponscleugh House
Allerwash, Fourstones
Hexham,
Northumberland
NE47 5AB
Tel: 01434 674271

Age Concern

Astral House
1268 London Road
Norbury London
SWI6 4ER
Tel: 0181 679 8000

National Association of Carers

20/25 Glasshouse Yard
London EClA 4JS
Tel: 0171 490 8818

MULTI-CULTURAL COMMUNITY

Ram Gidoomal, *Sari 'n' Chips* (Monarch Publications, 1993)

Church and Race – bulletin of CCBI Racial Justice Commission

Progress Within

C/o Cannon St Memorial
Baptist Church
300 Soho Road
Handsworth
Birmingham B21 9NA
Tel: 0121 551 5260

Reaching Out, Reaching In

C/o Battersea Chapel
Secretary's Tel: 0171 228 0393

Keyboard

1316 Ashley Road
St Paul's
Bristol BS6 5NU
Tel: 0117 941 4243

MELRAW
(a Methodist foundation offering training to churches in racism awareness)

56 Camberwell Road
London SE5 OEN
Tel: 0171 708 0676

Churches Commission on Racial Justice

CCBI
Inter Church House
35-41 Lower March
London SE1 7RL
Tel: 0171 620 4444

Evangelical Christians for Racial Justice

29 Trinity Road
Aston
Birmingham B6 6AJ
Tel: 0121 551 3885

DISABILITY

Faith Bowers (ed.), *Let Love Be Genuine* (Baptist Union of Great Britain, 1985)

Faith Bowers, *Who's This Sitting in My Pew?* (Triangle/SPCK, 1988)

Roger Grainger, *Strangers in the Pews* (Epworth Press, 1993)

David Pother, *Mental Handicap: Is Anything Wrong?* (Kingsway, 1993)

BUiLD Booklets – a series of four: *Knowing Jesus, Following Jesus, The Church, Joining the Church* (Baptist Union of Great Britain, 1991)

Torch Trust for the Blind
(Christian literature in Braille, giant print and cassettes)

Torch House
Hallaton
Market Harborough
Leicestershire LE16 8UJ
Tel: 0185 889 301

Fellowship for the Visually Handicapped
(supports Christian work amongst visually handicapped people worldwide. Compass Braille produces literature in Asian languages)

26 Cross Street
Moretonhampstead
Newton Abbot
Devon TQ13 8NL
Tel: 01647 40715

Agape Trust

118 Hastings Road
Battle
East Sussex TN33 OTQ
Tel: 01424 7773532

The Shaftesbury Society
(Christian care, education and accommodation for people with physical or learning disabilities)

18-20 Kingston Road
London SW19 lJZ
Tel: 0181 542 5550

BUiLD (Baptist Union initiative with people with learning difficulties)

12 Barford Crescent
Birmingham
B38 0BH
Tel: 0121 433 5417

CHAD
(Church Action on Disability)
(networking and information for churches)

Charisma Cottage
Drewsteignton
Exeter EX6 6QR
Tel: 01647 21259

Causeway
(promoting Christian awareness of and involvement with people with mental handicaps – produce videos)

P O Box 351
Reading
Berks RG1 7AL
Tel: 01734 508781

Carers Christian Fellowship

14 Yealands Drive
Ulverston
Cumbria LA12 9JB
Tel: 01229 585974

Carers National Association

20/25 Glasshouse Yard
London EClA 4JS
Tel: 0171 490 8818

Centre for Accessible Environments

35 Great Smith Street
London SWlP 3BJ
Tel: 0171 222 7980

MENCAP

National Centre
123 Golden Lane
London EC1Y ORT
Tel: 0171 454 0454

MIND

22 Hanley Street
London WlN 2ED
Tel: 0171 637 0741

National Federation of Families with Visually Impaired Children (LOOK)

Queen Alexandra College
49 Count Oak Road
Harbourne
Birmingham B17 9TG
Tel: 0121 428 2441

PECAN (Peckham Evangelical Churches Action Network)
(trains the long term unemployed, runs Employment Preparation courses, a Job Club and English language support for refugees)

2 Cottage Green
London
SE5 7ST
Tel: 0171 701 9844

Local Training and Enterprise Councils (TECs)
(offer schemes and retraining for unemployed people)

Details in telephone books or Job Centres

National Debtline
(offers advice and free booklets)

Tel: 0121 359 8501

Christian Outplacement Consultants and Trainers

Mr Derek Pratt
14 Broadlands
Holland Road
Frinton-on-Sea Essex
C013 9ES
Tel: 01255 677859

Revd Bryan Gilbert
22 The Bramptons
Shaw Swindon Wilts
SN5 9SJ
Tel: 01793 871958

CEPEC
(a commercial organisation which publishes a CEPEC Recruitment Guide listing around 7000 recruitment agencies in the UK)

CEPEC
Kent House
41 East Street
Bromley Kent BR1 lQC

The Executive Grapevine
(a service similar to CEPEC)

79 Manor Way
Blackheath London
SE3 9XG

UNEMPLOYMENT

John Atherton, *Christianity and the Market Place* (SPCK, 1992)

Julian Charley, *Pastoral Support for the Unemployed* (Grove Books)

Jon Davies, *God and the Market Place* (IEA, 1993)

Martyn Goss, *Where your treasure is* (Board for Chrstian Care, 1993)

Charles Handy, *The Future of Work* (Blackwell, 1984)

Jobsearch – a manual, written by Bryan Gilbert for Church Action with the Unemployed, containing material for a local church to organise its own Jobsearch Training Day.
Available from Next Step Training Services, 22 The Bramptons, Shaw, Swindon, Wilts SN5 9SJ.

Christians Unemployment Group from South Yorkshire (CHUG)

Raymond Draper
5 Church Lane
Wickersley
Rotherham
S Yorks S66 OES